THE ADDISON STREET ANTHOLOGY

BERKELEY'S POETRY WALK

EDITED BY ROBERT HASS AND JESSICA FISHER

HEYDAY BOOKS
BERKELEY, CALIFORNIA

Library of Congress Cataloging-in-Publication Data
The Addison Street anthology : Berkeley's poetry walk / edited by Robert Hass
and Jessica Fisher.
     p. cm.
  Includes index.
  ISBN 1-890771-94-5 (pbk. : alk. paper)
  1. American poetry—California—Berkeley. 2. Literary landmarks—California—
Berkeley. 3. Berkeley (Calif.)—Poetry. I. Hass, Robert. II. Fisher, Jessica.
  PS572.B4A33 2004
  811.008'0979467—dc22

                                               2004016993

Book design by David Lance Goines
Photograph on page x by Rebecca LeGates
Printing and Binding: United Graphics Inc., Mattoon, IL

Orders, inquiries, and correspondence should be addressed to:
        Heyday Books
        P. O. Box 9145, Berkeley, CA 94709
        (510) 549-3564, Fax (510) 549-1889
        www.heydaybooks.com

Printed in the United States of America

10 9 8 7 6 5 4 3 2 1

CONTENTS

NORTH SIDE *of* ADDISON STREET, *from* SHATTUCK *to* MILVIA

SOUTH SIDE *of* ADDISON STREET, *from* SHATTUCK *to* MILVIA

Sakai Harbor:
When ships from the foreign south
sailed to and fro
what a mingling of springs and
autumns there must have been

—Yosano Akiko, celebrating the diversity of the early days
of Sakai, her birthplace and now Berkeley's sister city,
translated by Janine Beichman

ACKNOWLEDGMENTS

The Addison Street Anthology was conceived by John Roberts, architect for the Addison streetscape design. The public art for the Downtown Addison Street Arts District was a project of the City of Berkeley Civic Arts Program, which is housed in the city's Office of Economic Development. Mary Ann Merker, the civic arts coordinator, provided steady leadership and unfailing enthusiasm as she shepherded the project through the city's offices and the Berkeley Arts Commission. Steve Huss served as public art consultant for the Addison streetscape and Scott Donahue was the technical consultant.

The downtown renovation and the creation of the arts district could not have occurred without the leadership of former mayor Shirley Dean, the support of current mayor Tom Bates, and the Berkeley City Council, the Berkeley Civic Arts Commission, especially Adam David Miller, and the support of the taxpayers of Berkeley through the Measure S Bond Issue. The design of the tiles was the work of David Lance Goines. Indispensable support came from Susie Medak, managing director of Berkeley Repertory Theater, and Malcolm Margolin of Heyday Books.

The costs of the fabrication and installation of the tiles were underwritten in part by financial contributions from many generous individuals, businesses, and organizations in Berkeley, including Avi and Dalia Nevo, David and Leigh Teece, Panoramic Interests, Patrick and Julie Kennedy, Reid and Susan Martin, ELS Architectural and Urban Designs, the University of California at Berkeley, the Wells Fargo Foundation, Ericsson, John and Jody Roberts, Oliver and Company Inc., the Trans Action Companies Ltd., the Aurora Theatre Company, the Bank of America, the Berkeley Art Center, the Berkeley-Sakai Sister City Association, Colliers International, councilmember Polly Armstrong, Gordon Commercial Real Estate, the 2001 Center Group, Joan Bardez, John and Barbara Papini, Michael Korman and Miriam Ng, Robbin Henderson, Seagate Properties Inc., SRM Associates, the Mechanics Bank, the Wareham Development Corporation, and the Jazzschool.

For research on the Peralta family, thanks to Holly Alonzo, director of the Friends of the Peralta Historical Hacienda Park in Oakland, and for information about Professor Kroeber's work with Ohlone speakers, to Andrew Garrett of the UC Berkeley linguistics department. Stephanie Manning, editor of *Shellmounder News,* was generous with her enthusiasm and her knowledge of the early days of West Berkeley. Linda Rosen of the Berkeley Historical Society was helpful, and Kenneth Cardwell of the Berkeley Architectural Heritage Association uncovered the poem about the Addison Street horse trolley. James Schevill, who knows the literary history of Berkeley better than anyone, was indispensable, as were some of the essays of the late Thomas Parkinson. Mitzi Sales and Helen Barber helped with the history of Berkeley Repertory Theater. Audrey Marrs did impeccable and efficient work as a project facilitator for Robert Hass.

Thanks are due, of course, to the poets for responding to our requests for biographical information and to poets and their publishers for waiving royalty fees so this project could occur.

The tiles were fabricated by the Cherokee Porcelain Enamel Corporation of Knoxville, Tennessee, and installed by the Berkeley Cement Company under the supervision of the City of Berkeley Public Works Department.

Everyone who worked on this project donated a good deal of personal time to it. Poems are one thing and tons of cast iron are another. When the panels arrived in the city's corporation yard from Tennessee, they needed to be lifted up, checked for damage, and accounted for, and this work needed to be done quickly. It got done on a succession of fall afternoons by Mary Ann Merker; John Roberts; Ted Burton, downtown coordinator for the Office of Economic Development; Melissa Wenzel, civic arts intern; Charlotte Fredriksen, civic arts staff; and Vincent Chen, assistant civil engineer for the City of Berkeley. They gave meaning to abstractions like "citizen involvement" and metaphors like "hands-on" and "heavy lifting."

Special thanks to Contee Seely for his assistance in facilitating the publication of this book. His appreciation of poetry was rekindled by Laurie Kuntz, to whom we also wish to express our gratitude.

INTRODUCTION

The Addison Street Anthology is a collection of poems, translations of poems, and song lyrics that reflect something of the social and literary history of Berkeley. Most of the poems were written by poets who were either born in the East Bay or lived and worked here for an important part of their lives. A few poets—like Robinson Jeffers of Carmel and George Oppen of San Francisco—are here because they have been so important to the development of poetry in California that they needed to be included to fill out the picture. A few poets just passed through, but their passing left a mark, and it is an aspect of the place that many gifted writers work here for a time, and the editors wanted the street to reflect that, too.

The work of the poets and playwrights in front of Berkeley Repertory Theater is there to tell another part of the story of the literary history of the city. Though William Shakespeare and Ben Jonson put in no time in the cafés of Telegraph Avenue, they have been, at least since the university's English department began mounting productions of Shakespeare in the new Greek Theatre in 1906, part of the city's cultural history. The song lyrics concentrated on the opposite side of the street are there for the same reason. Several translations have also been included because poets translate, and because Berkeley has always been a town full of gifted scholars, and they translate, and the translations have made a living presence of writers from many different eras and languages, and that also has been part of the story of poetry in the city.

Even people who think of themselves as aware of the liveliness of the literary scene here may be surprised by the sheer quantity and variety of the work represented in the Addison Street sidewalk. Prizes, of course, are not a measure of literary excellence. In fact, as an incubator of successive avant-gardes, Berkeley is the kind of place that has been apt to look with some suspicion at literary prizes. But it says something, at least, about the intensity of literary activity in the city to notice that an anthology of the history of its poets, lyricists, and playwrights includes two Nobel laureates in literature, two poets laureate of the United States, ten Pulitzer Prizes (counting three for Berkeley High graduate Thornton Wilder), three Obie Awards in drama, and almost two dozen National Book Awards and National Book Critics Circle Awards.

Of most of the history of song- and poem-making here, there is no record. People have probably been living on the east shore of San Francisco Bay for the last ten thousand years. Some of the most recent Native American inhabitants were an Ohlone people who spoke a language that the Spanish at the missions called Chochenyo. No songs in that language seem to have survived, but there are records of a few songs of nearby Ohlone peoples to give us the barest glimpse of pre-Conquest California. European culture began here in 1772 when a party of Spanish explorers sent out by the government of Mexico arrived in the vicinity of Strawberry Creek. (A plaque among the grove of redwoods at the edge of campus near Oxford and Center Streets marks the spot.) Some songs and poems from the brief flourishing of that culture came down to us in the papers of the Peralta family.

The town of Berkeley had its beginnings in 1873, the year the university moved to the Strawberry Creek campus, but it took a while for the new town and its provincial university to produce writing of interest. Nineteenth-century California had a few poets, but the most important literary event in the East Bay in the 1880s was probably the adolescent day-dreaming of Gertrude Stein in her family home in the Oakland hills. She would go east and then to Paris to make her literary career, and Thornton Wilder, who grew up in Berkeley in the tens of the century, would go to New York. Wilder sang in the choir at St. Mark's in Berkeley and took the Telegraph Avenue horse trolley to Oakland to see plays at the Liberty Theater. There may be more than a trace of Wilder's Berkeley in his portrait of the New England village in *Our Town*. That Berkeley was probably a wonderful place for a young boy to grow up, but it was not yet a town for writers. The portrait of the early city in Jack London's *Martin Eden*, published in 1909, suggests a culture that was staid, idealistic, and eminently respectable. The university's English and classical language departments offered poetry courses, and there was no doubt singing in the workingmen's taverns of Ocean View (not for long: Berkeley became dry in 1906, under the influence of the Women's Christian Temperance Union, and stayed that way until the repeal of prohibition in 1933), but it was not yet a culture to grow writers. Jack London, after trying a semester or two at UC, dropped out and headed for the goldfields of Alaska. George Sterling, the most talented poet of that generation, was not drawn to professorial Berkeley but to the new bohemian community developing in Carmel.

Poems do survive from that time—in the style of the newspaper verse of the period and printed locally. They give us a glimpse of the town in its early days. Here is one such piece from the archives of the Berkeley History Project. The poem, by J. Edward Boyd, was printed in a 1905 volume titled Ancient Poetry Revised and Modernised. It appears to be written in the manner of—or as a send-up of—Midwestern poets of the period who wrote nostalgic verses about their boyhoods among the cornfields.

In this case, the raw little town that is being cel-
ebrated is hardly twenty-five years old:

How dear to my heart are the scenes of my childhood,
Of pleasant old Berkeley that I used to know,
The gas tank, the planing mill, the old China wash-house,
The sweet-smelling mudholes where wild weeds did grow.

The old corner grocery store kept by Uncle Joe,
And his loud-talking driver who had such big feet;
The old Golden Sheaf where we bought coffee and sinkers,
And the poky old horse-car on Addison street.

How oft at the noon hour when the whistles loud did blow
Did I hasten home to eat a cold feed,
As I gaily sauntered down this well-beloved road,
How pleasant to smell the fragrant tar-weed.

But those bright days have gone, never more to come again—
Never more shall the sidewalk be trod by my feet,
Never more shall I see the bright scenes of my childhood
Or the poky old horse-car on Addison street.

How oft in my childhood I've "nipped" on the horse-car
To hear Mr. Morehead—How he did rip, curse, and swear,
And when he got done with his shouting and spouting,
He'd say, "You can't ride unless you have a nickel for fare."

But no more those bright days when the world looked so rosy.
This earth seemed a heaven and all things looked sweet.
But they've faded away, those bright scenes of childhood,
With the poky old cars on Addison street.

Real literary energy seems to have begun at the university with the brief instructorship in the late teens of a young Harvard graduate, Witter Bynner, who had edited his college literary magazine with his friend Wallace Stevens and had already begun to publish poems. Bynner had the novel idea of teaching a class in which students learned poetry by writing it. He received permission to proceed from the department chair and taught one of the first creative writing courses in the history of American higher education. Two young women in his class, Hildegarde Flanner and Genevieve Taggard, went on to publish books of poetry in the early twenties—the first by Cal graduates—and to establish literary careers. Bynner also met the newly arrived instructor in the Chinese language, Kiang Kang-hu, and, finding that they shared a passion for classical Chinese poetry, the pair embarked on what became a quite famous book of translations of T'ang Dynasty poetry. But Bynner was gone by 1920 and his presence seems not to have made a very lasting impression.

Or that is what one gathers from the report of a young Tennessean, Robert Penn Warren, who arrived in Berkeley in the fall of 1925 to do graduate work in English. Warren, who would become a poet and a novelist, author of *All the King's Men,* and one of the major Southern writers of the twentieth century, came from Vanderbilt, where there was already a flurry of literary activity around the new poetry of T. S. Eliot and Ezra Pound and the new fiction of Hemingway and Cather and Fitzgerald. He was going to be paid seventy-five dollars a month as an instructor while he worked on his master's degree. About the English department, he was discouraged: "They hadn't heard the news," he recalled, some years later. The professors had read Marx and Freud, but "I thought I was among the barbarians as far as poetic taste was concerned." Some of his friends from that time—they included an undergraduate girl, the future folk singer Malvina Reynolds—recall that he tried to repair the situation by standing up at a gathering of graduate students at a speakeasy in North Beach and, somewhat wobbly from the wonderful red wine that was beginning to be made from the vineyards of Sonoma County, recited the entirety of T. S. Eliot's *The Waste Land* from memory. Warren almost lost his job. The chairman of the English department at the end of his first year told him that he "exhibited an essential lack of enthusiasm for the work of teaching commercial English," but his friends on the faculty intervened, and in his second year he moved to a studio apartment on Telegraph Hill above a Spanish poolroom, commuted to the university on the ferry, soldiered on to the master's degree, and began to see his poems published in East Coast journals like the *New Republic.* A poem by Warren hasn't been included in the streetscape—there were so many stories to tell and his literary development was so rooted in the South—but he is also part of the city's literary record.

The Berkeley culture that was taking shape didn't come out of the graduate student bohemia of the 1920s, as might be expected. In the town, poetry was often the province of faculty wives, like Margaret Schevill, who was married to the professor of Spanish (at the time there was only one), or Henriette Durham, who was married at different times to two professors in the English department. There were not very many women faculty at the university in those years, but the cultural life of the town, as it grew from a population of 13,000 in 1900 to something like 65,000 in 1930, was carried on to a large extent by faculty wives and the wives of the business and professional class. In addition to women like Schevill and Durham, there were Theodora Kroeber and Louise Keeler, philanthropists Jane Sather and Phoebe Hearst, and the architect Julia Morgan and architects' wives Ada Coxhead and Annie Maybeck (a particularly fierce protector of native trees against developers). Other notable contributors to Berkeley's cultural life were Mary Keith, wife of the painter William Keith, and dancer Isadora Duncan's friend and disciple Florence Boynton, who produced free-form dance performances in Tilden Park. If professorial Berkeley looked staid to the young Jack London, it began to look different by the late teens and early twenties, when the area north of campus was referred to by folks in the flats as "Nut Hill." Many early Sierra Club members came out of the Berkeley hills and so did the Save the Redwood League and—in the person of Sylvia McLaughlin—the Save the Bay movement in the post–World War II years.

For the writers, a pair of events in the late 1920s and early 1930s were defining moments. Kenneth Rexroth arrived in San Francisco from Chicago in 1929, and a few years later Josephine Miles, born in Chicago but raised in Los Angeles, came to the university's English department to begin postgraduate studies in poetry. For forty years, from the mid-thirties through the mid-seventies, they would be the most influential teachers of poetry in the region, and between them—Rexroth with *In What Hour* in 1940 and Miles with *Local Measures* in 1946, they produced the first books of poetry by Bay Area writers that acquired a national readership and that are still read today.

Kenneth Rexroth was largely self-educated and a polymath. He was raised in the traditions of the Chicago socialism of the Progressive Era, had flirted with communism when he was in New York in his early twenties, was repelled by its authoritarian streak and its aesthetic conservatism, and arrived in San Francisco at the age of twenty-six an Episcopalian, a cubist in poetry and art, and an anarchist and social-ist of some kind, with an interest in French experimental writing, classical Greek litera-ture, and the art and culture of China. He set up as the city of San Francisco's resident bohemian artist and as he migrated spiritually from Christianity to Buddhism and from cubism to a kind of literary naturalism based on the example of classical Chinese poetry, he became everyone's teacher. He held a Friday night salon that drew several young Berkeley writers, broadcast programs on literature for Berkeley's listener-supported radio station KPFA, which he had helped found, wrote criti-cism for the literary magazines and a weekly column on literature and politics for the *San Francisco Examiner,* and wrote for the Sierra Club a practical book of instruction on camp-ing in the Sierra Nevada.

The other major figure of this period, Jose-phine Miles, was severely crippled by rheuma-toid arthritis and confined to a wheelchair even when she was a graduate student. She was an active scholar as well as a poet and produced a number of analytical books on style in the his-tory of English poetry. She must have been a fierce and determined spirit, but her friends comment mostly on her good humor and the brightness of her eye. The temper of her poems was plainspoken and classical. One of her friends, Harold Witt, wrote a sonnet about her that catches something of what she meant to

her students; it begins with an expression of surprise at his discovery of poems so well-made about such ordinary things:

JOSEPHINE MILES

What was this? Cornflakes in a poem?
And "neo-Spanish neatness of design"?
Not far from my surroundings there lived
    someone
Who sometimes said my very turn of mind.
Later up in Berkeley I would see her
Still young, already crippled, but with smiles
Shuffling through the hallway light of Wheeler,
A poet after my heart, Josephine Miles.

Then, though, I had only checked her out
And read her early wryness with delight—
Not a close and old acquaintance yet,
Only a starry shining in my night,
Who, if she had known me, would have said,
"Change that last line," or "Harold, it's all
    right."

Starting in the late 1930s and early 1940s there began to be enough writers to produce a literary culture, and the story gets richer and more complicated. There were the many poets whom Josephine Miles nourished, including James Schevill, who went on to direct the San Francisco Poetry Center; George P. Elliott, who wrote the most memorable fiction about

Berkeley in those years; and A. R. Ammons, a young North Carolinian who attended UC Berkeley in 1951 and 1952 to get a master's degree in English. Ammons became one of the most honored poets of his generation, but immediately after his three semesters in Berkeley, he went home to work in his wife's family's business and for years, he has said, his only lifeline to literature was his correspondence with Josephine Miles about his poems. Diana O'Hehir also studied with Miles in those years, and a very shy Barbara Guest took a literature course from her, as did so many young poets of the 1960s and 70s, including Susan Griffin and Barrett Watten.

In the mid-1940s a remarkable triumvirate of undergraduate poets—Robert Duncan, Jack Spicer, and Robin Blaser—arrived at the university. They were to become important figures in the postwar upsurge of new poetry associated with what got called variously the Beat generation and the San Francisco Renaissance. Duncan was part of Rexroth's salon, as was William Everson, a pacifist who had taken up printing while in a detention camp for conscientious objectors and who later became a lay Dominican monk at St. Albert's rectory in Oakland. Muriel Rukeyser, the already famous young left-wing poet from New York, dropped in on the Friday night sessions and skirmished with Rexroth about politics. Other members of Rexroth's circle included Thomas Parkinson

and Michael McClure, the first of whom would become an eminent critic of modern poetry, the other a poet of ecological imagination and a playwright who would scandalize audiences of the 1960s by putting onstage a mythic Billy the Kid doing something sexual to a mythic Jean Harlowe.

Robert Duncan, who became to the next generation of poets what both Rexroth and Miles had been to earlier ones, remembered the Berkeley of those years as a place where the air was alive with energies, both intellectual and erotic. His "A Poem Slow Beginning" from the breakthrough volume *The Opening of the Field* opens by

> remembering powers of love
>   and of poetry,
> the Berkeley we believed
>   grove of Arcady—
>
> that there might be
>   potencies in common things,
> "princely manipulations of the real"
>
> the hard electric lights,
>   filaments exposed
> we loved or studied by,
>   romantic,
> fused between glare and seraphic glow,
>   old lamps of wisdom
>   old lamps of suffering.

A grand synthesizer of romantic and modernist poetics, Duncan came to represent a different path from the matter-of-fact style of Josephine Miles, and, though they respected one another, in a time of uneasy relations between university English departments and literary avant-gardes, they came to stand for a town-gown division in the arts of those years. In the mid-1950s when the next wave of new poets arrived in the persons of Gary Snyder, a young man from Reed College who had come to study classical Chinese, and Allen Ginsberg, who had come from Columbia to study English, the mood was definitely more town than gown. Ginsberg decided against graduate school but stayed long enough to write several memorable poems about the city, including "A Strange New Cottage in Berkeley" and the much-anthologized "A Supermarket in California." His "Howl," written mostly in San Francisco, was the defining poem of the 1950s, and he performed it at a now-famous reading with Gary Snyder, Michael McClure, and Philip Lamantia at the Six Gallery in San Francisco, an event that was said to have announced the arrival of the Beat generation and that was chronicled by Jack Kerouac in his novel *The Dharma Bums.*

By 1960, Snyder and Ginsberg were gone, but they were legend enough to the counterculture of those years to have made both Berkeley and San Francisco destinations for young people from all over the country who dreamed of becoming writers. And, in the meantime, there were other unexpected arrivals. The university's Slavic languages department hired Czeslaw Milosz, a Polish poet living in France who had been a diplomat in the Communist government of postwar Poland before resigning and going into exile. Milosz was already famous then for his book *The Captive Mind,* on politics and literature in the Cold War. Thom Gunn, the youngest member of a group of postwar English poets that had become known as "The Movement," had studied poetry with Yvor Winters at Stanford before he was hired by UC Berkeley's English department, as were Peter Dale Scott, a Canadian diplomat with a degree in classics, and the Jamaican-born Louis Simpson, a prominent younger poet from New York.

These new arrivals did not constitute a group. Milosz, living on Grizzly Peak, writing poems in Polish about the sun setting over San Francisco Bay that were prohibited from being published in his country, can sound slightly dazed, in his poems from that time, by his isolation and the strangeness of his surroundings. "It is foggy," one of his poems goes, in the English translation, "so this must be July." He did find a literary friend in Peter Dale Scott, who had spent a year at the Canadian embassy in Krakow, and together they produced a volume of translations, *Postwar Polish Poetry,* that was to prove quite influential in the coming decades. American poetry had had a tendency to find the quickest route to transcendentalist affirmation; "Holy! Holy! Holy!" Allen Ginsberg's "Howl" had ended, though with a tinge of outraged irony. The poets that Milosz and Scott translated—poets who had survived the Holocaust, the Nazi occupation, and the Soviet seizure of their country—wrote from a deeper experience of fatality. "Maybe, maybe, maybe," these poems seemed to say, and young Americans were drawn to what seemed their grown-up sobriety in the seventies and eighties. Scott and Milosz also collaborated on a translation of another great Polish poet, Zbigniew Herbert, but their friendship cooled in the years of the Vietnam War demonstrations (as did the friendship between Robert Duncan and Denise Levertov). Scott, who wrote prose as well as poetry and had written a book about the unanswered questions in the assassination of President Kennedy, was an early activist in the antiwar movement. Milosz, who was no friend to American imperialism, kept his distance. His distrust of revolutionary communism was deep and instinctive. He belonged to the same generation as the Vietnamese leader Ho Chi Minh and other young provincial intellectuals who had been drawn to Paris in the 1930s and gotten their political education there. "We were many," he would write, "from Jassy and Koloshvar, Wilno and Bucharest, Saigon and Marrakesh,"

ready "to kill in the name of the universal, beautiful ideas." And this attitude must have deepened his isolation in the war years, when students in tie-dyed shirts were surging in the Berkeley streets and faculty were "dying in" on the chancellor's lawn to protest the university's weapons laboratories.

Meanwhile, Thom Gunn had settled in San Francisco. The poetic sensibility of postwar England had produced in his early work poems that were classical in technique, with an existential edge. In the United States of the 1950s, he was fascinated by the rebellious energy of the American young, the drag racers of Nicholas Ray's *Rebel Without a Cause*—an existentialist title, if ever there was one—and by James Dean's performance in that film, and the motorcycle-riding Marlon Brando of *The Wild One*. Gunn's book of poems from that time was called *The Sense of Movement*. He also found himself in the midst of another profound social change. His upper Market neighborhood, along Castro Street, was being transformed by the politics of gay liberation. When the young were coming to San Francisco—as the 1968 song went—with flowers in their hair, young gays and lesbians were finding in the Castro a village to live in with a freedom most of the rest of the country didn't offer. The arc of that movement—its ecstatic beginnings, its transformation into a political community after the assassination of gay political leader Harvey Milk, the devastation of the AIDS epidemic, and the community's recovery—is reflected, directly and indirectly, in Gunn's work, which is not about this movement but often observes the people and the forms of consciousness inside it. He was writing poetry very much his own, and not like anybody else's.

Louis Simpson, who arrived at the university in 1959, was born in the Caribbean, had served in the American infantry during World War II, and attended Columbia University in New York. He was also one of the editors of a poetry anthology published in those years entitled *New Poets of England and America*. The anthology, which aimed to represent the best new poets emerging in the postwar period, looks now—though it contains the work of many very important poets—extremely conservative in its approach. The entire explosion of new energy in American poetry—from Boston and New York and Chicago and San Francisco—was missing from the book. A Bay Area anthologist, Donald Allen, responded with a collection titled *The New American Poetry,* which included the Black Mountain poets—poets mostly from New England who had become associated with an experimental college in North Carolina—among whom were Robert Duncan, Denise Levertov, and Larry Eigner, who would come to figure in the literary history of Berkeley; also a group that came to be known as the Poets of the New York School (which included Berkeley graduate Barbara Guest); and the Beat generation. Into this last group Allen had lumped William Everson, then known as Brother Antoninus, the other two members of the Berkeley triumvirate, Jack Spicer and Robin Blaser, and a couple of younger poets who were then coming of age in San Francisco and were later part of the Berkeley literary scene, Ron Loewinsohn and David Meltzer.

In the years after, some literary historian would describe this as the period of the anthologies war. If it was a war, Louis Simpson was, for someone living in northern California, on the wrong side. And he seems not to have taken to Berkeley, though he wrote some of his best poems here and received the Pulitzer Prize for them while he was here. He had an outsider's ambivalence about the United States and he came to California—came "west," as the national mythology had advised—with Walt Whitman in mind at the tail end of the postwar suburbanized 1950s. His book of those years was called *At the End of the Open Road;* "Walt," he wrote, "the open road leads to the used car lot." Simpson seems never to have been comfortable in Berkeley; he wrote a novel while he was here about New York City, *Morningside Drive,* and he seems to have returned to New York without regret. He was another kind of Berkeley writer: the one who didn't take.

Miles and Rexroth, Duncan and Spicer, Ginsberg, Snyder, Milosz, Scott, Gunn, Simpson: from the days of the early gatherings of handfuls of poets, such as there are in most small and large American cities, sharing poems and occasionally getting up magazines, Berkeley and the Bay Area had become a place of many different literary currents and of many writers going their own ways, doing the quiet and mostly private work of pursuing their muses and shaping bodies of work. The city, of course, and the country, were changing in those years. The military bases and the war industries, like the shipyards in Richmond and Oakland, had brought large numbers of African Americans to the East Bay, and many of them stayed. There began to be a black blues-club scene in Oakland and, in the 1950s, a bohemian venue of folk music clubs and dark wineshops along San Pablo Avenue with names like Siddhartha and The Blind Lemon.

It would not be inaccurate to describe the social look of the postwar East Bay by saying that black people lived in the poorer housing west of Sacramento Street, that students, some African American families, and some middle-class whites mingled in the upper flatlands, and that white people of the professional class lived in the Thousand Oaks district, in the Claremont area, and in the hills. These were years of ice loosening. The demonstrations against McCarthy and the House Un-American Activities Committee had carried their energy into the civil rights movement. Berkeley was in the process of integrating its public schools. The civil rights movement had fed the campus uprising of the free speech movement, and the free speech movement became the basis of the peace movement in the Vietnam years. This was the time when Berkeley got its international reputation as the template of social turbulence and change.

Some of the poets reflected this process and some didn't. In 1967 the young African American poet and novelist Ishmael Reed arrived, also to teach at the university. Reed would meet a University of Michigan graduate, Al Young, another poet and novelist, who was taking a second bachelor's degree in Spanish, and together they launched a magazine called Yardbird, which aimed to reflect the diversity of the actual culture that was evolving outside the university. An early feminist press named Shameless Hussy appeared in Oakland, and in Berkeley there emerged a more experimental women's press, Kelsey Street. Within a few years a monthly calendar began to appear just to keep track of all the poetry readings in the Bay Area. The calendar quickly evolved, in the hands of Joyce Jenkins, into the tabloid newspaper *Poetry Flash,* which has become an institution in the Bay Area's literary culture. A Poets' Cooperative, modeled on the city's grocery co-op and its cheese-selling co-op and its cooperative bakeries and its wine-making equipment co-op (called, in the Berkeley manner, Wine and the People, as if to conjure a socialist utopia of hand-crafted cabernets), was meeting and publishing books in the 1970s. Many small experimental presses sprouted up in the 1980s along with another generation of experimental writers.

And Berkeley had become a city of bookstores. There was, first of all, Fred Cody's and then Andy Ross's Cody's Books, which had been founded as a new kind of retail enterprise in the 1950s, selling paperback books to students. And there was Moe's Used Books next door. And University Press Books, founded by Bill and Karen McClung in the 1970s. There was Peter Howard's and Jack and Vicki Shoemaker's literary bookstore, Sand Dollar Books, and Amy Thomas's Pegasus and Pendragon. Black Oak Books sprang up on the northern end of Shattuck Avenue around the time that the literature student drop-outs who had founded new businesses out of a discovered love of food and cooking had turned those blocks into what came to be known as the Gourmet Ghetto. Peter Howard would shift his operation to Serendipity Books on University Avenue, and Small Press Distribution, a company developed to distribute to bookstores all the new small press writing, opened a retail outlet on San Pablo Avenue. In the 1980s came Diesel Books in Rockridge. The

bookstores, and the reading series in the bookstores, at the colleges and universities, and in the cafés, became—like the city's good bread and good coffee, its restaurants and outdoor flower stalls, its famous but fitful concern with social and environmental justice—part of Berkeley's culture.

The story of the poetic part of that culture has become in the last few decades as thick and complicated as an interesting root system should be. Almost half of the poems now embedded along Addison Street were written after 1970 and they represent only a snapshot of the literary activity during those years, when poetry wasn't—though it had never entirely been—a special province of the university. For one thing, writing programs had sprung up at the California College of Arts and Crafts, at Mills College and St. Mary's and UC Davis. And poetry has become as much an activity of the city as of its institutions of learning. Among the poets represented in these more recent years there are many professors of English and of creative writing, but there are also a carpenter, a psychiatrist, an administrator for the Social Service Administration, a librarian, two psychotherapists, the director of a science museum, technical writers, business people, and computer technology specialists. Many other poets might have been included in the street.

Another block could have been given to the art of translation—from Lyn Hejinian's translations of the post-Soviet Russian poet Arkadii Dragomoshchenko, to Kay Richards's translations of modern Korean poetry, to Candace Slater's translations of Brazil's most popular poet, Manuel Bandeira, to translations of the odes of Horace by Jake Fuchs (better known in town as a soccer coach), and translations by Chana Bloch and Marcia Falk of the Song of Songs. There is more poetry in the air—and it is drawn from more times and places—than one can easily see or represent.

Berkeley is a city of walkers. There was a time when strolling Telegraph Avenue to browse its book and record and print stores, followed by coffee at the Caffe Mediterraneum, was a date. Almost all Berkeleyans walk the pier once in a while, which is also a date, especially on evenings in September and October when the fog hovers offshore and gives the city its long Indian summers. And everyone has their favorite hike in Tilden Park, whether it is the long stroll along the ridge at Inspiration Point, or the hike out Wildcat Creek or up Strawberry Canyon, or the long winding walk toward Grizzly Peak on the trail behind Clark Kerr campus. Birders—two of the poets in the street wrote books about field ornithology—walk the Berkeley Marina in the early morning or just before sundown to watch the terns diving and feeding or to spot black-crowned night herons or a rarer green heron stand utterly still along the bank. There

are walkers of the upper reaches of Spruce Street and Euclid Avenue on evenings in February when the plum trees are in blossom. This walk ends at the Rose Garden, where one can sit on a bench and watch the sun go down over Tamalpais and the Golden Gate. The UC Botanical Gardens is a walk, and so is the Tilden Native Plant Garden, where Berkeleyans show up in throngs once a year on Saturday mornings for the annual native plant sale. The University Center for Forestry prints a map of rare trees on the campus, and that is another date: an afternoon's walk looking for ginkgos and Italian stone pines and incense cedars from the Sierra Nevada, and from China the almost extinct dawn redwood (after which you have a bowl of steaming noodles at a student café on Euclid Avenue).

The Saturday morning farmer's market on Center Street is a stroll, and there is the university's art museum to walk in (with a whole floor of Hans Hoffman's paintings from the abstract expressionist era), and the Lawrence Hall of Science in the hills, and an anthropology museum, and a Jewish museum. In North Berkeley, the neighborhoods were laid out with paths cutting through their winding streets, so it is possible to climb from the flats to the hilltops on neighborhood paths. The merchants of Solano Avenue hold every fall an organized stroll to promote their shops and restaurants, and in the family neighborhoods of Elmwood east of College Avenue, the front yards that transformed into haunted houses and trick-or-treat labyrinths at Halloween had become so inventive in the 1980s and 90s that even Berkeleyans who weren't trailing small children turned out to watch. There is a dog-walking park along Hearst, and the upscale shops of Fourth Street in what used to be the town of Ocean View, where walkers can still hear the trains going past and smell the Pacific in the air, is also a walk. Lately a citizens' group has been promoting the idea that the city should daylight Strawberry Creek from the western edge of the campus where it goes underground to the shore of San Francisco Bay, reopening the stream, the ecosystem, and the conversation between the bay and the hills that Strawberry Creek conducted for eons before the twentieth century paved it over. That would be another of the city's walks.

The Addison Street Anthology was conceived in the spirit of walking. Once the architect of the downtown renewal project, John Roberts, had imagined an installation of art and poetry in the Addison Street sidewalk, and once the first committee decided that poems reflecting the history of writing in the city might be a good idea, there was the question of whether to do whole poems or—as has been done in other cities—a series of quick takes, pithy quotations, or memorable phrases. An argument for this approach was that

streets are made for getting from here to there. Sound bites from poems might be more striking to people in a hurry. Another argument was that whole poems—all short enough, twenty or so lines, to fit the space of a tile—would not necessarily be the best way to represent the poets. Another argument was that it was asking a lot of a small city to produce one hundred good poems in a century. There were centuries, like the fifteenth, one member of the committee remarked, in which the whole of England did not produce fifty poems that people still want to read. The arguments for complete poems, rather than catchy fragments, were two. The first was that if you want to represent poets in the practice of their art, and their art is making poems, then you have to represent them with whole poems. The second argument was that if you filled a street with more than one hundred entire poems, people would have to come back often and walk the street slowly over time if they were going to take them in. It would be a way to spend, from time to time, part of an afternoon or a summer evening. The final decision favored strolling.

Then a material for the tiles had to be chosen. The tiles in the street are cast iron. A dark charcoal when they were installed, over time the tiles will oxidize and change color toward a deep rust. The lettering is porcelain enamel, which looked bright white against the black iron when installed but should eventually become a warm ivory against the rust-colored metal. The typographical design of the poems needed to be simple, elegant, and readable, and artist David Lance Goines provided it. Once the poems were chosen, they needed to be put in order. This task fell to the editors of this book, who chose to place the poems in roughly chronological order down both sides of the street, with some slight effort to put writers of the same generation near one another. A strict chronological tracking, therefore, would require some hopscotching back and forth across the street. There are theater poems for people standing in line or loitering at intermission in front of Berkeley Repertory Theater, and music lyrics and poems about music in the future vicinity of the concert venue Freight and Salvage. The younger poets are on the west end of the street near the students at Berkeley High, from whom some part of the next century of Berkeley poems will come. The tiles begin on the north and south sides of Addison at Shattuck with Ohlone songs.

Those Indian songs seemed an appropriate symbolic place to begin, not only because the Ohlone people are the oldest culture that we know about that lived here, but also because of the way their songs came into our possession. Once a university was established here, one of its tasks became to ask questions about its surroundings. That was what sent Alfred Kroeber, then twenty-seven years old and a newly minted professor of anthropology, to Monterey in April of 1901. He took a train to Watsonville, and a stagecoach to Monterey, and when he asked Maria Soto and Jacinta Gonzales to sing their songs, it was a way of saying: Tell me something about who you are. Tell me something about what it has been like to live in this place.

—Robert Hass
Berkeley, California
July 2004

15

NORTH SIDE *of* ADDISON STREET, *from* SHATTUCK *to* MILVIA

See! I am dancing!
On the rim of the world I am dancing!

—Ohlone song

This song was collected from a seventy-eight-year-old Ohlone woman, Maria Viviana Soto (1823–1916), in Monterey in 1901 by Alfred Kroeber, the university's first professor of anthropology. In April of that year, hearing of a group of surviving Ohlone speakers in the Monterey peninsula, Kroeber took a train to Salinas and a stagecoach to Monterey, where he heard and transcribed this song. Maria Soto spoke Rumsien, the language of the Ohlone people who lived from south of San Jose to Big Sur. The Ohlones in the Berkeley area spoke the somewhat different but closely related Chochenyo language. One of their villages was located at what is now the corner of Claremont and Telegraph Avenues.

Professor Kroeber (1876–1960) was born in Hoboken, New Jersey, and educated at Columbia University. In 1901 he established the anthropology department at the university and he is considered one of the founders of modern anthropology. He educated generations of Berkeley students and is the author of numerous books including *Handbook of the Indians of California.* He is probably best remembered as the man who brought to the Bay Area the Yahi Indian Ishi, the last surviving member of his northern California people. Kroeber's wife, Theodora, is the author of the now classic book about Ishi's life, *Ishi in Two Worlds.*

Now then,
you will all dig for roots—
They are already getting ripe.
Let us climb sugar pines!
We shall move out at dawn.
You will set up camp.

Now then,
I shall go climbing for pine nuts—
All the people will move out there.
We shall all set up camp there.
There is a good spring.
Perhaps others will be arriving too.
We shall wait for them, what do you say?

Now then,
Let us climb for them.
Bring food along!

Now then,
some of you will dig for tiger lilies.

Now then,
gather food for winter!
You women will probably want to dig instead of climb.
If you should succeed in this—
well then, we will all get winter food.

   —Yana song

The Yana were a mountain people of northern California. The language they spoke belongs to the Hokan family. This song is originally in a variant of the Yahi dialect of Hokan spoken by Ishi, the last surviving Yahi Indian. The Yana suffered early and hard at the hands of white settlers and miners. Three thousand strong at the time of contact, they were all but wiped out in 1864 in one of the most comprehensive and brutal massacres in California history. The linguist and ethnographer Jeremy Curtain, visiting in 1884, was able to locate only thirty-five native speakers of the language, which is now extinct.

This text was collected by anthropologist and linguist Edward Sapir and published in his *Yana Texts* in 1910. It was sung for Sapir in 1907 by a Yana woman named Betty Brown (whose Yana name was C'iidaymiya). A Northern Yana speaker, she was working as a washerwoman when Sapir met her. He paid her $1.50 a day to teach him Yana and tell him stories and songs. This song comes from a traditional story; the speaker is a legendary figure named Young Buzzard, who was a Yana chief.

Being idle in the wooden building, I opened a window.
The morning breeze and bright moon lingered together.
I thought of my native village far away, cut off by clouds and mountains.
On the little island the wailing of cold, wild geese can be faintly heard.
The hero who has lost his way can talk meaninglessly of the sword.
The poet at the end of the road can only ascend a tower.

—anonymous Chinese immigrant detained at Angel Island

From 1910 to 1940, Angel Island in San Francisco Bay was the point of entry for most of the 175,000 Chinese immigrants who came to America in those years. It was also a detention center for immigrants awaiting the outcomes of medical examinations and the inspection of their documents. The United States in the late nineteenth century had passed a number of laws aimed at curbing Asian immigration, the most infamous of which was the Chinese Exclusion Act of 1882. There were, however, loopholes in the law and by the early twentieth century economic conditions in China had become sufficiently hard that many Chinese tried to get into the United States in the hope of finding a better life. The unofficial policy of the Immigration Service was to make entry difficult by assuming that all Chinese documents were suspect. This led to long, frustrating detentions in wooden barracks on a hillside that looked across the bay to San Francisco. Over the years, many of the immigrants wrote poems on the walls of those barracks. This is one of those pieces. A collection of the poems was transcribed and translated by Him Mark Lai, Genny Lim, and Judy Yung in *Island: Poetry and History of Chinese Immigrants on Angel Island, 1910–1940*. The barracks have been preserved and can be visited at Angel Island State Park.

COPA DE ORO (THE CALIFORNIA POPPY)

Thy satin vesture richer is than looms
    Of Orient weave for raiment of her kings!
    Not dyes of olden Tyre, not precious things
Regathered from the long forgotten tombs
Of buried empires, not the iris plumes
    That wave upon the tropics' myriad wings,
    Not all proud Sheba's queenly offerings,
Could match the golden marvel of thy blooms.
For thou art nurtured from the treasure-veins
    Of this fair land; thy golden rootlets sup
    Her sands of gold—of gold thy petals spun.
Her golden glory, thou! on hills and plains,
  Lifting, exultant, every kingly cup,
    Brimmed with the golden vintage of the sun.

   —Ina Coolbrith

24

Ina Coolbrith (1841–1928) was *the* poet of Victorian California. Born Josephine Smith in Nauvoo, Illinois, she was the niece of Joseph Smith, founder of the Mormon Church. Her father died when she was an infant, and her mother, fleeing anti-Mormon violence, remarried, to an attorney named William Pickett, who took the family to California. Josephine Pickett—she had taken her stepfather's name—would recall, many years later, whiling away hours in the back of a covered wagon as it rumbled across the plains, reading her stepfather's leatherbound edition of the poems of Lord Byron. The family came over Beckwourth Pass to Marysville in late September of 1851. Within two years they had moved to San Francisco, and in another two to Los Angeles, when the town was still more Mexican than American. Coolbrith grew up there, began to write poetry, had a young girl's social life—she remembered dancing at a ball with Don Pio Pico, California's last Mexican governor—and married at the age of seventeen. She was divorced at nineteen from her violent and erratic young husband and moved with her family to San Francisco in 1862. There she fell in with Bret Harte, the editor of California's newest literary magazine, *Overland Monthly*, and became, along with Harte and the magazine's principal contributor, Charles Stoddard, one of the triumvirate that made up literary San Francisco in the 1860s.

Coolbrith found a job teaching school and made a life around the magazine. In 1871 she was invited to compose a commemorative ode on the occasion of the third graduation ceremony at the new University of California. Five years later, when the university had moved to Berkeley, she composed another poem for the 1876 graduation, at which, for the first time, two women were numbered in the graduating class. She became a librarian for the Oakland Public Library in 1874 and continued in that position until 1893, when she was fired by the board's trustees for insubordination. She then moved back to San Francisco and became a librarian at the Mercantile Library.

Her poems have come to seem quite old-fashioned, but during these years she was one of the best-known literary figures in California. Her friends included most of the writers and artists in northern California at the time—John Muir, the painter William Keith, Gertrude Atherton, Ambrose Bierce. She encouraged the young Jack London, a newsboy from the Oakland streets who came into the library to read, and she became a mentor to Mary Austin, author of the classic book of the California desert, *The Land of Little Rain*. The state legislature honored her with the title of California Poet Laureate in 1915. In her last years she moved to a cottage on Wheeler Street in Berkeley, where she died in 1928. A park on Russian Hill in San Francisco and an undergraduate literary prize at UC Berkeley bear her name.

TRIOLET

He came in
　　When I was out,
To borrow some tin
Was why he came in,
　　And he went without;
So I was in
　　And he was out.

　　—Jack London

26

Jack London (1876–1916) was born in San Francisco and brought up by his mother and John London, whom she married when her son was an infant. The family moved to Oakland when Jack was six. John London opened a grocery, which did not prosper, and Jack helped support the family by selling newspapers on the street. He also haunted the Oakland Public Library, where one librarian, the poet Ina Coolbrith, encouraged his literary interests. After teenage adventures on San Francisco Bay in the fish patrol and as an oyster pirate, he sailed to the waters north of Japan as a deckhand on a seal-hunting ship. When he returned, he crammed for the entrance exam to the University of California, without having finished high school. He was admitted and dropped out after his first semester. In 1897 he joined the gold rush to the Klondike and put the experience to use when he published his Alaskan stories and *The Call of the Wild* in 1903. Among his best books are *The Sea-Wolf* (1904) and *Martin Eden* (1909). "Triolet" was first published in a magazine in 1908 and later reprinted in *Martin Eden,* a novel about an Oakland writer. In chapter 22, the young working-class hero recites the poem to his upper-middle-class Berkeley girlfriend, saying, "It's not art, but it's a dollar." She replies, "I want the man I love and honor to be something finer and higher than a perpetrator of jokes and doggerel." "Tin" is slang for "cash."

THE BLACK VULTURE

Aloof upon the day's immeasured dome,
    He holds unshared the silence of the sky.
    Far down his bleak, relentless eyes descry
The eagle's empire and the falcon's home—
Far down the galleons of sunset roam;
    His hazards on the sea of morning lie;
    Serene, he hears the broken tempest sigh
Where cold sierras gleam like scattered foam.

And least of all he holds the human swarm—
    Unwitting now that envious men prepare
    To make their dream and its fulfillment one,
When, poised above the caldrons of the storm,
    Their hearts, contemptuous of death, shall dare
    His roads between the thunder and the sun.

    —George Sterling

George Sterling (1869–1926) was the best-known California poet of the early years of the century. Born in Sag Harbor, New York, his family sent him to Oakland in 1890 to learn his uncle's real estate business. He quickly learned the literary life of the Bay Area instead, becoming friends with Jack London and Ambrose Bierce. His first book of poetry, *The Testimony of the Suns*, appeared in 1903. Sterling moved to Carmel in 1905 and met Robinson Jeffers there. He committed suicide in 1926 by taking cyanide in his room at the Bohemian Club in San Francisco. Although Sterling published ten volumes of poetry, he is best remembered as the sensitive, heavy-drinking poet on whom Jack London modeled the character of Martin Brissenden in *Martin Eden*.

CARMEL POINT

The extraordinary patience of things!
This beautiful place defaced with a crop of suburban houses—
How beautiful when we first beheld it,
Unbroken field of poppy and lupin walled with clean cliffs;
No intrusion but two or three horses pasturing,
Or a few milch cows rubbing their flanks on the outcrop rockheads—
Now the spoiler has come: does it care?
Not faintly. It has all time. It knows the people are a tide
That swells and in time will ebb, and all
Their works dissolve. Meanwhile the image of the pristine beauty
Lives in the very grain of the granite,
Safe as the endless ocean that climbs our cliff. —As for us:
We must uncenter our minds from ourselves;
We must unhumanize our views a little, and become confident
As the rock and the ocean that we were made from.

   —Robinson Jeffers

Robinson Jeffers (1887–1962) was born in Pittsburgh and grew up in Los Angeles. He arrived in Carmel in 1914, where for the next half century he wrote poems about California that came to define a West Coast tradition. He also wrote plays, and one of them, *The Tower Beyond Tragedy*, was performed by the university's drama club in the Greek Theatre in 1932, a time when his twin sons, Garth and Donnan, were attending the school.

LOVERS

From somewhere over the houses, through the silence,
Through the late night, come windy ripples of music.
There's a lighted cigarette-end in the black street,
Moving beside the music he has brought her.
Behind a shuttered window, there's a girl
Smiling into her pillow. And now by her hand
There's a candle lighted and put out again.
And the shadow of a bird leaves its perch for a smaller twig.

   —Witter Bynner

Witter Bynner (1881–1968) played a brief but crucial role in the literary life of Berkeley. Born in New York and raised in New England, he attended Harvard, where he was a classmate of Wallace Stevens. He went to work as a magazine editor in New York and came to Berkeley to teach literature at the university in 1918. Bynner's impressions of Berkeley are conveyed in a letter written from the Hotel Carleton in July 1919:

> Living in Berkeley is like living in Brooklyn—except that Berkeley is beautiful and satisfying—it sequesters you. Only one weekend have I had off for tramping. I rode up and walked down Tamalpais on the most crystal day of the year. From its top came a sprig of wild lilac which I enclosed in a box for you and some acacia. The latter dries gracefully and lasts in my room for weeks. I hope it reached you not too much shaken, an odd little gray-green ghost from a countryside which sings with changing bloom. The fruit trees!—it has been almost like Japan.

In the spring semester of 1919 Bynner taught what is thought to be the first creative writing class to be offered at an American university. He began, he said, with "thirteen girls and fourteen boys and plenty of blank paper." His students included three Berkeley undergraduates, Genevieve Taggard, Stanley Coblentz, and Hildegard Flanner, who became well-published American writers. It was also at Berkeley that Bynner met Kiang Kang-hu and began with him their immensely influential translations of classical Chinese poetry. Bynner left Berkeley in 1920 to travel in China and later settled in Santa Fe, New Mexico.

DRINKING ALONE WITH THE MOON

From a pot of wine among the flowers
I drank alone. There was no one with me—
Till, raising my cup, I asked the bright moon
To bring me my shadow and make us three.
Alas, the moon was unable to drink
And my shadow tagged me vacantly;
But still for a while I had these friends
To cheer me through the end of spring....
I sang. The moon encouraged me.
I danced. My shadow tumbled after.
As long as I knew, we were boon companions.
And then I was drunk, and we lost one another.
....Shall goodwill ever be secure?
I watched the long road of the River of Stars.

—Li Po, translated by Witter Bynner and Kiang Kang-hu

Li Po (701–762) is regarded as one of the greatest of all Chinese poets. Legend has it that he drowned while "drinking alone with the moon."

Witter Bynner met Kiang Kang-hu in Berkeley in 1918. Kiang came from a prominent family and served in several government posts, including secretary to the president of China's provisional government, Yuan Shih-k'ai. He was also an organizer and head of the Chinese Socialist Party. One of the young people who worked for him as an office assistant was Mao Tse-tung. When Yuan began to maneuver himself into being declared emperor, Kiang made the scheme public and had to flee for his life. He became the first instructor of Chinese language at the university.

Bynner had spent the previous year in China and Japan. Drawn together by common interests, he and Kiang began to collaborate on the translations of classical Chinese poetry that eventually became *The Jade Mountain,* one of the classics of American literary translation. Later Kiang returned to Shanghai, where he founded Southern University. During World War II, catastrophically, he took the position of Minister of Education in the puppet government set up by the Japanese at Nanking. After the war he was sentenced to death for treason by the Nationalist government. Partly through the intervention of Bynner and other friends, his sentence was commuted to life imprisonment. The Communist government that followed the Nationalist one did not revoke the sentence. He died in prison in Shanghai on December 6 or 7, 1954.

TIME OUT

We will put Time to sleep on that warm hill.
Lie naked in the tawny grass and fill
Our veins with golden bubbles.
                                        Grass will grow
Beneath your arm-pits and between your feet
Before we take our bodies up, and go
Like dazzled aliens through the dusty street.

   —Genevieve Taggard

Genevieve Taggard (1894–1948) grew up in Hawaii, where her missionary parents had moved from Washington State to found a public school. The family moved to Berkeley in 1914, where Genevieve attended the university. She studied poetry with Witter Bynner and edited the literary magazine, *Occident.* After graduation she moved to New York, where she worked for a publisher and served as editor of the influential journal *New Masses* in the 1920s. Her first book of poems, *For Eager Lovers*, was published in 1922. She also founded a poetry magazine and wrote a pioneering biography of Emily Dickinson. In her later years, a conservative in poetry and a radical in politics, she taught at Bennington and Sarah Lawrence and lived on a farm in Vermont.

MOMENT

I saw a young deer standing
Among the languid ferns.
Suddenly he ran—
And his going was absolute,
Like the shattering of icicles
In the wind.

—Hildegarde Flanner

Hildegarde Flanner (1899–1987) was born in Indianapolis, Indiana. She attended Sweet Briar College in Virginia for a year and then transferred to Berkeley, where she found her way into Witter Bynner's creative writing class. After graduation she moved to New York; her first volume of poems, *Young Girl*, was published there in 1920. She returned to Berkeley and settled into a house with her mother. The house burned down in the Berkeley fire of 1923. She married in 1926 and moved to southern California, where she continued to write and publish poetry. Over the years she spent a good deal of time in Paris, where her sister Janet Flanner, a well-known writer for the *New Yorker* magazine, lived. In 1962 she moved to the Napa Valley, and in 1985 she published a collection of essays, *Brief Cherishing*. She died in St. Helena.

ANDRÉE REXROTH

died October, 1940

Now once more gray mottled buckeye branches
Explode their emerald stars,
And alders smoulder in a rosy smoke
Of innumerable buds.
I know that spring again is splendid
As ever, the hidden thrush
As sweetly tongued, the sun as vital—
But these are the forest trails we walked together,
These paths, ten years together.
We thought the years would last forever,
They are all gone now, the days
We thought would not come for us are here.
Bright trout poised in the current—
The raccoon's track at the water's edge—
A bittern booming in the distance—
Your ashes scattered on this mountain—
Moving seaward on this stream.

   —Kenneth Rexroth

Kenneth Rexroth (1905–1982) was born in South Bend, Indiana, and grew up in Chicago. He arrived in San Francisco with his wife, Andrée, in 1927. Rexroth came with a passion for mountains, radical politics, classical Chinese and Japanese poetry, Christian and Asian mysticisms, and European avant-garde literature. These interests came to define the San Francisco tradition and made him a presiding presence at the birth of the Beat generation. His first book, *In What Hour*, was published in 1940. In the 1930s and 40s he was at the center of what cultural life there was in the Bay Area. During World War II his was one of the few voices raised against the forced detention of Japanese Americans, and immediately after the war he organized the Libertarian Circle to discuss literature and anarchism. Among the members of this informal group were Robert Duncan, Jack Spicer, Muriel Rukeyser, William Everson, and Tom Parkinson. Out of it came the idea for KPFA, a cooperatively-run, listener-sponsored radio station. The founders were Lewis Hill, Richard Moore, and Eleanor McKinney. Beginning in 1950, Rexroth made weekly trips to Berkeley for over a decade to broadcast literary and political commentary on this pioneering alternative station. In his later years he taught poetry at UC Santa Barbara.

SUMMER, THE SACRAMENTO

To this bridge the pale river and flickers away in images of blue.
And is gone.   While behind me the stone mountains
stand brown with blue lights;   at my right shoulder standing
Shasta, in summer standing, blue with her white lights
near a twilight summer moon, whiter than snow
where the light of evening changes among these legends.

Under me islands lie green, planted with green feathers,
green growing, shadowy grown, gathering streams of the green trees.
A hundred streams full of shadows and your upland source
pulled past sun-islands, green in this light as grace,
risen from your sun-mountains where your voices go
returning to water and music is your face.

Flows to the flower-haunted sea, naming and singing, under my eyes
coursing, the day of the world.   And the time of my spirit streams
before me, slow autumn colors, the cars of a long train;
earth-red, earth-orange, leaf, rust, twilight of earth
stream past the evening river and over into the dark of north,
stream slow like wishes continuing toward those snows.

   —Muriel Rukeyser

Muriel Rukeyser (1913–1980) was born in New York City and grew up there on Riverside Drive. She attended Columbia and Vassar. Her first book of poetry, *Theory of Flight*, was published in 1935 when she was twenty-two years old. After the war, in early 1946, she moved to Berkeley and taught a course at the California Labor School in Oakland. She was married briefly—the marriage was annulled after a few months—and gave birth to a son, whom she raised on her own. When she was feeling quite desperate for money, an anonymous benefactor left her a yearly allowance—$1,200 to be paid on the first of the year—and advised her to raise her child and write her poems. Rukeyser never knew the identity of her patron, but it turned out to be her friend, Henriette de S. Blanding, another Berkeley poet. Rukeyser gave up the allowance when she returned to New York in 1954 to teach at Sarah Lawrence. A prolific writer, poet, essayist, feminist, biographer, and translator, she taught several generations of young women writers, among them Alice Walker. She died in New York City.

REASON

Said, Pull her up a bit will you, Mac, I want to unload there.
Said, Pull her up my rear end, first come first serve.
Said, Give her the gun, Bud, he needs a taste of his own bumper.
Then the usher came out and got into the act:

Said, Pull her up, pull her up a bit, we need this space, sir.
Said, For God's sake, is this still a free country or what?
You go back and take care of Gary Cooper's horse
And leave me handle my own car.

Saw them unloading the lame old lady,
Ducked out under the wheel and gave her an elbow,
Said, All you needed to do was just explain,
Reason, reason is my middle name.

   —Josephine Miles

Josephine Miles (1911–1985) was born in Chicago and moved to southern California when she was five. She received a BA from UCLA in 1932 and then a PhD in English from Berkeley. In 1940 she became an instructor in Berkeley's English department. Severely disabled most of her life by arthritis, she was a beloved and central teacher of young Berkeley poets from the 1940s to the 1970s. Her disability seems to have made her an alert and wry observer of the world. This poem doesn't directly say that it's from the point of view of a handicapped woman who needs to be carried from a car—it doesn't need to. What interested Miles was human beings and how to capture them in the plain, tart, direct language that she loved.

THERE ARE MANY PATHWAYS TO THE GARDEN

If you are bound for the sun's empty plum
there is no need to mock the wine tongue
but if you are going to a rage of pennies
over a stevedore's wax ocean
then, remember: all long pajamas are frozen dust
unless an axe cuts my flaming grotto.

You are one for colonial lizards
and over bathhouses of your ear
skulls shall whisper
of a love for a crab's rude whip
and the rimless island of refusal shall seat itself
beside the corpse of a dog
that always beats a hurricane
in the mad run for Apollo's boxing glove.

As your fingers melt a desert
an attempt is made to marry the lily-and-fig-foot dragon
mermaids wander and play with a living cross
a child invents a sublime bucket of eyes
and I set free the dawn of your desires.

The crash of your heart
beating its way through a fever of fish
is heard in every crowd of that thirsty tomorrow
and your trip ends in the mask of my candle-lit hair.

   —Philip Lamantia

Philip Lamantia was born in San Francisco in 1927. In the years just after World War II a poetry scene was beginning to emerge in Berkeley. One of its centers of energy was *Circle,* a magazine edited by George Leite, owner of a local bookstore, and designed by the visual artist Bern Porter. *Circle,* which first appeared in mimeograph form with the blessings of Kenneth Rexroth and Henry Miller, was antiwar, antiauthoritarian, and committed to new art, especially French surrealism. Lamantia, just nineteen years old, was already an ardent surrealist. He published in early issues of the magazine, and when Leite and Porter started a press, the first book they published, in 1946, was Lamantia's *Erotic Poems.* In the following year Lamantia and Sanders Russell started a rival San Francisco avant-garde journal, *The Ark.* Robert Duncan would remark later, shrugging off the Berkeley–San Francisco rivalry, "We were all brought up on Daddy Rexroth's reading list." Lamantia went on to publish many books; City Lights published his *Selected Poems 1943–1966* in 1967 and *Bed of Sphinxes*, a collected poems, in 1997.

WINTER PLOUGHING

Before my feet the ploughshare rolls the earth,
Up and over,
Splitting the loam with a soft tearing sound.
Between the horses I can see the red blur of a far peach orchard,
Half obscured in drifting sheets of morning fog.
A score of blackbirds circles around me on shining wings.
They alight beside me, and scramble almost under my feet
In search of upturned grubs.
The fragrance of the earth rises like tule-pond mist,
Shrouding me in impalpable folds of sweet, cool smell,
Lulling my senses to the rhythm of the running plough,
The jingle of the harness,
And the thin cries of the gleaming, bent-winged birds.

   —William Everson

William Everson (1912–1994), also known as Brother Antoninus, was born in Sacramento, grew up in the San Joaquin Valley, and apprenticed himself to the poetry of Robinson Jeffers. A poet, a printer, and a conscientious objector during World War II, he also became a lay monk in the Dominican Order and lived for many years at St. Albert's Priory in Oakland. He was at the same time a chief figure in the San Francisco Poetry Renaissance of the 1950s. In his later years he left the order—stripping his monk's robes at a poetry reading at UC Davis in 1969—and taught poetry at UC Santa Cruz. This poem is from his early years of farm work in the San Joaquin and gets something of the feel of that life in the 1920s, when fields were still turned by horse and plow.

THE STRUCTURE OF RIME II

What of the Structure of Rime? I said.

    The Messenger in guise of a Lion roard: *Why does man retract his song
from the impoverishd air? He brings his young to the opening of the field.
Does he so fear beautiful compulsion?*

I in the guise of a Lion roard out great vowels and heard their amazing patterns.

A lion without disguise said: He that sang to charm the beasts was false
of tongue. There is a melody within this surfeit of speech that is most
man.
    What of the Structure of Rime? I asked.

    *An absolute scale of resemblance and disresemblance establishes measures
that are music in the actual world.*

    The Lion in the Zodiac replied:

    *The actual stars moving are music in the real world. This is the meaning of
the music of the spheres.*

    —Robert Duncan

Robert Duncan (1919–1988) was born in Oakland, went to UC Berkeley, where he edited a magazine of new writing, *Experimental Review*, and became a seminal figure in the San Francisco Renaissance, along with his classmates Robin Blaser and Jack Spicer. He lived most of his life in San Francisco and Stinson Beach with his companion, the painter Jess. As a young poet Duncan published a pioneering essay on civil rights for homosexuals in the influential magazine *Politics*, which led to his being banned from several East Coast academic journals. His style mixed, grandly, the high visionary language of Romantic poetry with the experimental techniques of modernism. He made poetry itself and the powers of imagination one of his central subjects, as he does in his sequence of poems "The Structure of Rime," from which this piece is taken. His stepfather was an architect and Duncan was fascinated by the way the imagination makes forms, "as if," he wrote, "it were a given property of the mind that certain bounds hold against chaos." He was also a famously brilliant talker and enormously influential among the young poets of Berkeley and San Francisco.

A TEXTBOOK OF POETRY, 21

Hold to the future. With firm hands. The future of each afterlife, of each ghost, of each word that is about to be mentioned.

Don't say put beauty in here for the past, on account of the past. On account of the past nothing has happened.

Stick to the new. With glue, paste it there continually what God and man has created. Your fingers catch at the edge of what you are pasteing.

You have left the boys' club where the past matters. The future of your words matters. That future is continually in the past.

That pathology leads to new paths and pathfinding. All the way down past the future. The words go swimming past you as if they were blue fish.

—Jack Spicer

Jack Spicer (1925–1965) was born in Los Angeles and in 1944 came to UC Berkeley, where he studied linguistics and met Robert Duncan and Robin Blaser, with them constituting the Berkeley poetry scene in those years. In the 1950s he taught a "Poetry as Magic" workshop in a San Francisco bar and organized Blabbermouth Night, spontaneous poetry readings at The Place in North Beach. The outsider's outsider, he remained aloof from most of the social life of the San Francisco Renaissance and the Beat generation poets. He died of alcoholism at the age of forty.

CUPS #5

The intensities
of these branches
of willow
open.

What is it
broke the skin?

How lovely
that jewel
of under the skin.

Neither dark nor light
is my true love.

The blood whose beauty crosses
the hand like money
will fight for that true love.

   —Robin Blaser

Robin Blaser was born in Denver, Colorado, in 1925. He went to Northwestern University and then in 1944 transferred to Berkeley, where he met Robert Duncan and Jack Spicer and studied history with Ernst Kantorowicz, poetry with Josephine Miles, and philosophy with Hannah Arendt. He left Berkeley with Jack Spicer in 1956 to become a librarian at Harvard University. They returned to San Francisco in 1959, and in 1966 Blaser took a job at Simon Fraser University in Vancouver, where he taught for twenty years and still lives. His many books of poems were collected in *The Holy Forest*, published in 1993. A book about Blaser, *Even on Sunday*, was edited by Miriam Nichols and published in 2002; it includes some of his reminiscences about the now-legendary literary scene in Berkeley in the 1940s.

PRE-TEEN TROT

We trot hand-in-hand in the morning
Down where the huge ocean hums.
Both of us wear striped bikines
To cover our neat little bums.

Blythly we trot in the morning
As far as the Boardwalk extends,
Wearing the same striped bikines
Because we are intimate friends.

But my stripes are brighter than your stripes,
This every watcher must know,
Broader and brighter than your stripes,
When we trot where the sea breezes blow.

 —Helen Adam

Helen Adam (1909–1993) was born in Glasgow, Scotland. She attended Edinburgh University and worked as a journalist in London. In 1939 she moved to New York and from there to San Francisco in 1948, where she met Robert Duncan and Robin Blaser and became part of a group that met to share poems. An actress, playwright, and poet, her first American books were in ballad form: *The Queen o' Crow Castle* in 1958 and *Ballads* in 1961. She made her living for a while, as her friend Madeline Gleason did, as a message runner in the San Francisco Stock Exchange. Her play *San Francisco's Burning*, written in collaboration with her sister Pat Adam, was produced in Berkeley in 1963. She published a book of stories about witchcraft and brought out—from small publishers with names like Toothpaste Press and Hanging Loose—several more books of the eccentric songs, ballads, and poems that her Berkeley friends had admired. She also acted in several experimental films, and her life is the subject of a documentary by the filmmaker Rosa von Praunheim. Adam died in Brooklyn, New York. "Bikine" is her spelling of the name of the brief swimming suit that came into fashion in the 1950s, a name derived from the Pacific atoll where the atomic bomb was tested.

A STRANGE NEW COTTAGE IN BERKELEY

All afternoon cutting bramble blackberries off a tottering brown fence
under a low branch with its rotten apricots miscellaneous under the
leaves, fixing the drip in the intricate gut machinery of a new toilet;
found a good coffeepot in the vines by the porch, rolled a big tire out
of the scarlet bushes, hid my marijuana;
wet the flowers, playing the sunlit water each to each, returning for
godly extra drops for the stringbeans and daisies;
three times walked round the grass and sighed absently:
my reward, when the garden fed me its plums from the form of a
small tree in the corner,
an angel thoughtful of my stomach, and my dry and lovelorn tongue.

—Allen Ginsberg

Allen Ginsberg (1926–1997) was born in New Jersey and spent only a few years in the Bay Area, but his first book, *Howl*, was written here and it, together with his Columbia classmate Jack Kerouac's novel, *On the Road*, launched the Beat movement. Ginsberg first came to California for graduate school in English at UC Berkeley, but he dropped out after a few weeks. In this poem, written in 1965, he is, like generations of students before him and after, settling into new and unfamiliar living arrangements in the early fall. Here he is also trying out the long verse line, full of casual observation and attention to the present moment, that would form the basis of his later work.

THE PLUM BLOSSOM POEM

Angel island.
The sailboat slipping barely west,
Floating over coiling
                    tongues of filling mud.
East face of the Sierra still is
                    tilting;
Two plums below Buchanan street
                    on Vallejo
Blow blossom petals
                    eastward down the walk.
We hold and caress each other
Where a world is yet unborn;
Long slow swells in the Pacific—
                    the land drifts north.

   —Gary Snyder

Gary Snyder was born in San Francisco in 1930 and raised in Washington and Oregon. One of the founding figures of the Beat movement, he attended Reed College and did graduate study in Asian languages at UC Berkeley before moving to Kyoto to study Zen Buddhism. He won the Pulitzer Prize for poetry in 1975 and has been described as the twentieth century's Thoreau. There is a lightly fictionalized portrait of Snyder and Allen Ginsberg living in Berkeley in Jack Kerouac's novel *The Dharma Bums*. From 1986 until 2002, Snyder taught poetry at UC Davis. He lives in the Sierra Nevada foothills near Grass Valley.

SONG

                    I WORK WITH THE SHAPE
                         of spirit
                      moving the matter
                        in my hands;
                              I
                           mold
                          it from
                      the inner matrix.
                    Even a crow or fox
                       understands.

—Michael McClure

Michael McClure was born in Marysville, Kansas, in 1932 and grew up in Seattle and Wichita. He attended the University of Wichita and the University of Arizona, coming to San Francisco in 1955, where he studied poetry with Robert Duncan at San Francisco State University and became a member of Kenneth Rexroth's Friday night meetings. He gave his first public reading at the Six Gallery event in 1955 at which Allen Ginsberg first read "Howl." A playwright as well as a poet, he received an Obie Award for *The Beard,* which was produced in 1965 in San Francisco and 1967 in New York. In those years, living in the Haight-Ashbury neighborhood, he also wrote the lyric "Mercedes Benz" for Janis Joplin and a book about the Hell's Angels, *Freewheelin' Frank.* His books of poems include *Ghost Tantras, September Blackberries,* and *Jaguar Skies.* He has taught for many years at the California College of Arts and Crafts and lives in the Oakland hills.

PARACHUTES, MY LOVE, COULD CARRY US HIGHER

"I just said I didn't know,
now you are holding me in your arms,
how kind."
Parachutes, my love, could carry us higher.
Around the net I am floating,
pink and pale blue fish are caught in it,
they are beautiful, but they are not good for eating.
Parachutes, my love, could carry us higher
than this mid-air in which we tremble.
Having exercised our arms in swimming,
now the suspension, you say,
is exquisite. I do not know.
There is coral below the surface, there is sand and berries
like pomegranates grow.
This wide net, I am treading water
near it. Bubbles are rising and salt
drying on my lashes, yet I am no nearer
air than water. I am closer to you
than land, and I am in a stranger ocean
than I wished.

—Barbara Guest

Barbara Guest was born in Wilmington, North Carolina, in 1920 and grew up in Los Angeles. She came to Berkeley in 1939, where she took a class with Josephine Miles but remembers being too shy to speak to her. She graduated from the university in 1943, moved to New York City, where she befriended the poets Frank O'Hara, John Ashbery, and James Schuyler, and became associated with the poets and painters who constituted the "New York School" in the 1950s and 60s, especially the women painters Jane Freilicher, Helen Frankenthaler, Joan Mitchell, and Grace Hartigan, who were emerging at that time. She wrote about painting for *Art News* in the 1950s and published her first book of poems, *The Location of Things*, in 1960. She has since published more than twenty volumes of poetry, a novel *(Seeking Air)*, a biography of the poet H. D., and essays on literature and painting. In the 1990s Guest moved back to Berkeley, where she lives in a cottage on Milvia Street and is a revered and influential figure on the poetry scene. The Poetry Society of America awarded her the Robert Frost Medal for Distinguished Lifetime Work in Poetry in 2001.

from **COLD MOUNTAIN POEMS**

The path to Han-shan's place is laughable,
A path, but no signs of cart or horse.
Converging gorges—hard to trace their twists
Jumbled cliffs—unbelievably rugged.
A thousand grasses bend with dew,
A hill of pines hums in the wind.
And now I've lost the shortcut home,
Body asking shadow, how do you keep up?

   —Han Shan, translated by Gary Snyder

Han Shan, whose name means "Cold Mountain," was a famed Buddhist poet and recluse of the T'ang dynasty (618–907). Not much is known of his life, except what can be learned from his poems. His work reflects an outsider tradition in classical Chinese and Japanese poetry, a tradition of irony, humor, spiritual freedom, social criticism, and an ideal of voluntary simplicity in wild places. Han Shan's stance is echoed in the Japanese monk-poet Saigyo, who is said to have lived for a season on brookwater and fallen chestnuts while he meditated and wrote poetry.

Gary Snyder began these translations while he was studying at UC Berkeley with the great T'ang scholar Edward Schaeffer (who pronounced his student a "better than average" scholar of intermediate Chinese.) A fictionalized account of Snyder's discovery of Han Shan is recorded in Jack Kerouac's *The Dharma Bums*, a book that became a sort of bible to the backpacking hippies of the Vietnam era and that made an old Asian spiritual and artistic tradition available to young people in the United States.

noise absorbed
      in the air

   happiness
      is quiet

    have fun,   they say

     the birds lean on bark
       and sing
           to our ears

   —Larry Eigner

Larry Eigner (1927–1996) was born in Lynn, Massachusetts, and lived in nearby Swampscott until he was fifty-one. Born of a Yiddish-speaking immigrant family, he suffered from severe cerebral palsy, brought about by an injury at birth, and was confined to a wheelchair all his life. His career as a poet began when he heard the poet Cid Corman talking about new stirrings in American poetry on a Boston radio station in 1949. Eigner was soon in correspondence with Corman and sending poems to a magazine edited by another Massachusetts poet, Robert Creeley. In 1953 Creeley's press at Black Mountain College in North Carolina published Eigner's first book, *From the Sustaining Air*. In the late 1970s his work was of interest to a younger group of experimental poets, who published it in the first issue of their magazine, *L=A=N=G=U=A=G=E*. After the death of his father in 1978, Eigner moved to California, where another young poet, Robert Grenier, became his friend and caretaker and helped him to prepare typescripts of his poems. Eigner became a regular at Berkeley's many poetry readings in the 1980s and early 1990s, much admired for his poems and his connection to the Beat poets and the New York and Boston experimental poets of an earlier generation. He died in Berkeley.

from **NOTEBOOK**

Thursday, May 15th, 1969—Berkeley

At 6 a.m. the ominous zooming, war-sound, of helicopters breaks into our sleep.

To the Park:
ringed with police.
Bulldozers have moved in.
Barely awake, the people—
those who had made for each other
a green place—
begin to gather at the corners.

Their tears fall on sidewalk cement.
The fence goes up, twice a man's height.
Everyone knows (yet no one yet
believes it) what all shall know
this day, and the days that follow:
now, the clubs, the gas,
bayonets, bullets. The War
comes home to us…

   —Denise Levertov

Denise Levertov (1923–1997) was born in England, the daughter of an English mother and a Russian Jewish father who was an Anglican priest. She was educated at home and published her first book of poems, *The Double Image*, in 1946. Around that time, she met a young American writer, Mitchell Goodman, in Paris, married him, and moved to the United States. It was through her correspondence and friendships with two West Coast writers, Kenneth Rexroth and Robert Duncan, that she became associated with the new postwar poetry in America. Her second book, *Here and Now*, was published by Lawrence Ferlinghetti's City Lights Books. Levertov was active in the peace movement and taught in UC Berkeley's English department as a visiting poet at the time of the largest anti–Vietnam War demonstrations and the struggle over People's Park. "Notebook," a poetic journal she kept of that period, was reprinted in *Relearning the Alphabet* in 1970 and was refashioned as part of the long poem "Staying Alive," which appeared in *To Stay Alive* in 1971. Levertov lived at various times in New York, Mexico City, Boston, and rural Maine. In the late 1980s and early 1990s she taught half the year at Stanford, and then spent her last years in Seattle. A prolific writer, she published many volumes of poetry and prose and translated the French poet Eugene Guillevic. She had many friends in Berkeley, including the poet and psychotherapist David Shaddock, Susan Griffin, her old friend Robert Duncan, and Czeslaw Milosz, and her visits were almost always the occasion for a party.

Sleeplessness. Homer. The sails tight.
I have the catalogue of ships half read:
That file of cranes, long fledgling line that spread
And lifted once over Hellas, taking flight.

Like a wedge of cranes into an alien place—
The gods' spume foaming in the princes' hair—
Where do you sail? If Helen were not there
What would Troy matter, men of Achaean race?

The sea, and Homer—it's love that moves all things.
To whom should I listen? Homer falls silent now
And the black sea surges toward my pillow
Like a loud declaimer, heavily thundering.

    —Osip Mandelstam, translated by Robert Tracy

Osip Mandelstam (1891–1938) is one of the great Russian poets of the twentieth century and notoriously difficult to translate. He was a contemporary of Boris Pasternak and Anna Akhmatova. Akhmatova and Mandelstam were united in aiming for a hard, clear, classical poetry. Their movement came to be known as Acmeism. Mandelstam was arrested in 1934 for writing an epigram against Josef Stalin and he died in the gulags. His first book, *Kamen'*, from which this poem comes, is a landmark of Russian poetry. Robert Tracy's translation of it, *Stone,* was published in 1981. Tracy is a professor of English and Celtic studies at UC Berkeley and a scholar of Irish literature. He was born in 1928 and studied English and Russian literature at Harvard. His critical books include *Trollope's Later Novels* and *The Unappeasable Host: Studies in Irish Identities.*

DYING IN

dying on the grass
in front of the chancellor's building
for Charlie Schwartz's anti-weapons protest

brings back confused
memories of the wartime sixties
hitting the dirt before we realized

these were just wooden bullets
and then walking back through tear gas
to teach a class

lying here
and watching the neutral passers-by
scale the vertical asphalt

I feel neither
the old embarrassment at being
at right angles to most people

with brief-cases
nor, and this is the spooky part
that steam of comprehending anger

only the warm
smell of the grass beside my nose
saying, *come back here every now and then*

 —Peter Dale Scott

Peter Dale Scott was born in Montreal in 1929. He was educated at McGill University and did graduate work at Oxford. After four years in the Canadian diplomatic service, during which he spent some time in Warsaw, he came to Berkeley in 1961 and taught in the speech and English departments. At Berkeley he became friends with Czeslaw Milosz and together they translated the great Polish poet Zbigniew Herbert. Scott was an activist in the years of the anti–Vietnam War movement and a scholar of the underside of American politics. In addition to short poems and a trilogy of long poems about private life and political violence in the twentieth century *(Coming to Jakarta, Listening to the Candle,* and *Minding the Darkness),* he wrote a study of the assassination of John F. Kennedy *(Deep Politics and the Death of JFK)* and another of the CIA's involvement in the cocaine trade *(Drugs, Oil and War).* The poem included here remembers a bit of political theater in which UC Berkeley faculty lay down like dead bodies on the chancellor's lawn to protest the university's involvement, through its Livermore laboratory, in the production of weapons; it also describes the atmosphere on campus during the Vietnam protests when police used tear gas and wooden bullets to disperse protesters.

THE NIGHT PIECE

The fog drifts slowly down the hill
And as I mount gets thicker still,
Closes me in, makes me its own
Like bedclothes on the paving stone.

Here are the last few streets to climb,
Galleries, run through veins of time,
Almost familiar, where I creep
Toward sleep like fog, through fog like sleep.

    —Thom Gunn

Thom Gunn (1929–2004) was born in Gravesend, England, and educated at Trinity College, Cambridge, where he began to publish and became associated with a British group of postwar poets known as "The Movement." He came to California in 1954 to study poetry at Stanford with Yvor Winters and began teaching at UC Berkeley in 1958. He became, over his forty years as a teacher at Berkeley and as a San Francisco resident, an acute observer of life in northern California, especially the emergence of the gay community in San Francisco's Castro District. He is considered one of the most important literary presences in the Bay Area in the second half of the century. The author of more than twenty volumes of poetry, he has had a long association with Berkeley's literary magazine of the 1980s and 90s, *The Threepenny Review,* and its editor Wendy Lesser. He received a MacArthur fellowship and many other literary honors in both England and the United States. Throughout the Bay Area's many years of literary and social experimentation, most of his poems maintained, in a seemingly effortless and casual way, a classical sense of form.

from **THE TEMPEST**

Our revels now are ended. These our actors,
As I foretold you, were all spirits and
Are melted into air, into thin air;
And, like the baseless fabric of this vision,
The cloud-capped towers, the gorgeous palaces,
The solemn temples, the great globe itself,
Yea, all which it inherit, shall dissolve
And, like this insubstantial pageant faded,
Leave not a rack behind. We are such stuff
As dreams are made on, and our little life
Is rounded with a sleep.

   —William Shakespeare

William Shakespeare (1564–1616) was an English playwright of the late sixteenth century. His plays must have been produced in Berkeley, or passages from them declaimed, almost as soon as the Strawberry Creek campus opened in 1873. Beginning in 1906, the English club at the university began an annual series of Elizabethan plays at the Greek Theatre, and Shakespearean productions at Berkeley High probably followed not long after—in 1914 the young Thornton Wilder had a small part in the drama club's production of *As You Like It*. Berkeley Repertory Theater did its first productions of Shakespeare in its second season: they staged *The Merry Wives of Windsor* in the eighty-seat theater at College and Ashby, directed by Michael Leibert, and alternated with *Twelfth Night*, directed by Robert Mooney. Over the years the Rep has staged *Julius Caesar, Love's Labour's Lost, The Comedy of Errors, Much Ado About Nothing, Hamlet, The Merchant of Venice, As You Like It, Measure for Measure, The Winter's Tale, Macbeth,* and *Antony and Cleopatra*. The city's appetite not slaked for the stuff dreams are made on, Berkeleyans have performed Shakespeare in their parks at least since Charles Keeler staged a play at Live Oak Park in the 1920s. The California Shakespeare Festival began as a summer night performance of *A Midsummer Night's Dream* in John Hinkel Park in 1974, and now produces multiple plays each year.

PROLOGUE *to* EPICOENE

The ends of all, who for the scene do write,
    Are, or should be, to profit, and delight.
And still't hath been the praise, at all best times,
    So persons are not touched, to tax the crimes.
Then, in this play, which we present tonight,
    And make the object of your ear and sight,
On forfeit of yourselves, think nothing true:
    Lest so you make the maker to judge you.
For he knows, poet never credit gained,
    By writing truths but things (like truths) well feigned.
If any, yet, will (with particular sleight
    Of application) wrest what he doth write;
And that he meant or him, or her, will say;
    They make a libel, which he made a play.

—Ben Jonson

Ben Jonson (1573–1637) was an English poet and playwright of the late sixteenth and early seventeenth centuries. He was a friend of William Shakespeare, and the fiercest satirist of the Elizabethan stage.

Berkeley Repertory Theater began in 1968 when Michael Leibert, a graduate student in directing at the university, mounted a production of Georg Buchner's *Woyzek* at International House. He called his ensemble "The Pomegranate Players." The play drew a crowd; emboldened, he rented an empty grocery store on College Avenue near Ashby, put in eighty seats (old couches and folding chairs), and remounted the show. Though the new company was playing at first to houses of five or six patrons, the Elmwood neighborhood eventually took them in, and the theater became a cultural center and an alternative to movies. People could walk to the theater, bring their children, get to know the actors. Leibert soon changed the name to Berkeley Repertory Theater. Berkeley Rep was conceived as a professional Actors Equity company, and it began with a core of ten actors who needed to be paid. By 1977 neighborhood involvement had transformed itself into tangible action. The theater had a managing director in the person of Mitzi Sales. Helen Barber helped create a board of directors while the theater continued its adventurous string of productions, sometimes with sets made out of cardboard boxes. The pioneering members of the board that gave the city what eventually became one of the preeminent repertory theaters in the country were Ed Shiver, Karl Kardel, Narsai David, Patsy Mote, Henry Kaiser, Martha Hertelendy, Bob Oliver, and Garen Staglin. It is not a story that Ben Jonson—who specialized in witlessness, vanity, and greed—could have done very much with. But the world continued to provide enough of it for the theater to mount, over the years, successful performances of *Volpone* and *The Alchemist*.

from **OUR TOWN**

The First Act was called the Daily Life.
This Act is called Love and Marriage.
There's another Act coming after this:
I reckon you can guess what that's about.

—Thornton Wilder

Thornton Wilder (1897–1975), one of America's foremost playwrights and the author of *Our Town*, *The Skin of Our Teeth*, and *The Matchmaker*, was born in Madison, Wisconsin. He went to Hong Kong as a child when his father was appointed U.S. consul to China, but later moved to Berkeley with his mother and siblings to be educated at home. He lived on the corner of Parker and College and attended Emerson School. His mother helped make costumes for university performances at the new Greek Theatre, and the children had walk-on parts in several productions, including a turn as Medea's children. The family attended the First Congregational Church, but Thornton, who was fascinated by the organ there, became a choir boy at St. Mark's Episcopal Church. His sister remembers him having to slip out of the Congregational service early to race up the street to the Anglican Church of which his father, a New England Yankee, did not approve. The children returned to China for a year and then came back to California, where in 1913 Thornton entered Berkeley High. The family was living on Prospect Street near the horse-trolley line that led directly to the Liberty Theater in Oakland, which produced a repertory of melodramas and farces to which the young Wilders resorted as often as they were allowed. Thornton also got to see the great actress of the era, Sarah Bernhardt, perform in the Greek Theatre. At the high school he had a small part in Shakespeare's *As You Like It* and began to write one-act plays. After his graduation in 1915, he attended Oberlin College, interrupted his studies to serve in an artillery battalion in World War I, returned to graduate from Yale, and received an MA from Princeton. His first play was produced in 1926, and he received the Pulitzer Prize in fiction for *The Bridge of San Luis Rey* in 1928. He also received the Pulitzer Prize in drama in 1938 and 1943. He taught at Lawrenceville Preparatory School in New Jersey from 1921 to 1928 and at the University of Chicago from 1930 to 1936, and he served in Army Air Intelligence during World War II.

EPILOGUE *to* THE GOOD WOMAN OF SZECHWAN

You're thinking, aren't you, that this is no right
Conclusion to the play you've seen tonight?
After a tale, exotic, fabulous,
A nasty ending has slipped up on us.
We feel deflated too. We too are nettled
To see the curtain down and nothing settled.
How could a better ending be arranged?
Could one change people? Can the world be changed?
Would new gods do the trick? Will atheism?
Moral rearmament? Materialism?
It is for you to find a way, my friends,
To help good men arrive at happy ends.
You write the happy ending to the play!
There must, there must, there's got to be a way!

   —Bertolt Brecht, translated by Eric Bentley

Bertolt Brecht (1898–1956) was one of the leading German playwrights of the twentieth century, a politically committed poet, and the inventor of a new epic theater. *The Good Woman of Szechwan* was written between 1939 and 1941 while Brecht, in exile from Nazi Germany, was living and working in Sweden. The play was first produced in Zurich in 1942.

Berkeley Repertory Theater performed it as *The Good Person of Szechuan*, directed by Sharon Ott and Timothy Near, in the 1986–87 season. A production of Brecht's *Galileo*, directed by Michael Leibert, opened the new Addison Street theater in 1980, and Tony Taccone directed *The Caucasian Chalk Circle* in the 1994–95 season. In 1997 Taccone became artistic director and the Rep received a Tony Award for Outstanding Regional Theater. The earliest Rep production of Brecht was Michael Leibert's *Mann Ist Mann,* staged at the College Avenue theater in 1976–77.

from **FOR COLORED GIRLS WHO HAVE CONSIDERED SUICIDE / WHEN THE RAINBOW IS ENUF**

      she waz sullen
      & the rhinestones etchin the corners
              of her mouth
      suggested tears
      fresh kisses that had done no good
she always wore her stomach out
lined with small iridescent feathers
the hairs round her navel seemed to dance
& she didnt let on
she knew
from behind her waist waz achin to be held
the pastel ivy drawn on her shoulders
waz to be brushed with lips and fingers
smellin of honey & jack daniels

   —Ntozake Shange

Ntozake Shange was born Paulette Linda Williams in Trenton, New Jersey, in 1948. When she was eight, her family moved to St. Louis, where she was bused to a predominantly German American public school in enforcement of the U.S. Supreme Court's 1954 ruling on *Brown v. Board of Education*. She finished high school back in New Jersey, attended Barnard College, and did graduate work in American Studies at the University of Southern California, receiving an MA in 1973. In 1971 she changed her name to Ntozake Shange, a name derived from the Xhosa language of South Africa. She moved to the Bay Area and taught at Sonoma State College, Mills, and UC Extension, recited poetry at the Third World Collective, and danced with Raymond Sawyer's Afro-American Dance Company and the West Coast Dance Company. In the summer of 1974 she began work on a series of poems patterned on Judy Grahn's *The Common Woman* and, through experiment, transformed her poem/collage into a theatrical work. *For Colored Girls Who Have Considered Suicide / When the Rainbow Is Enuf* was first performed at the Bacchanal, a woman's bar in Oakland, and published by Alta's Shameless Hussy Press in 1975. The play moved to off-Broadway and then Broadway, where it ran for two years and received an Obie Award and Grammy and Emmy nominations. It has been in repertory ever since. Shange now lives in Philadelphia and continues to write poems and plays. She has taught in the theater programs at Yale University and New York University.

from **HYDRIOTAPHIA**

Happily I turn the earth,
tunnelling for all I'm worth.
Who needs heaven, who needs souls?
Below is Paradise for moles...
Heaven's bright and full of fluff,
and never is there dirt enough,
so heaven's not where moles are found
but digging deeper
deeper deeper
always deeper underground....

—Tony Kushner

Tony Kushner was born in New York City in 1956. His parents, both classical musicians, moved the family to Lake Charles, Louisiana, where he grew up. He graduated from Columbia University in 1978 and got an MFA in directing from the theater program at New York University in 1984. His first full-length play, *A Bright Room Called Day*, premiered in San Francisco in 1987. This led to a commission from the Eureka Theater in San Francisco for the play that eventually became *Angels in America,* which won the Pulitzer Prize for drama in 1993. Kushner's relationship with Berkeley Rep began with Sharon Ott's staging of his adaptation of Pierre Corneille's *The Illusion* in 1990–91. Since then, the Rep has staged *Slavs!,* directed by Tony Taccone in 1995–96, and *Hydriotaphia,* directed by Ethan McSweeney in the 1998–99 season, during which Kushner spent some time at the theater, meeting audiences and talking to students from the university. Tony Taccone directed his *Homebody/Kabul* in the 2001–02 season.

SPRING HARVEST OF SNOW PEAS

They're taller than me.
I taste and eat as I pick along,
choose the flat big ones and baby ones,
and leave the bulging pods for shelling or seed.
The purple and lavender blossoms
and the blue blossoms wave above me
and touch my neck.
I stand on the ledge of the box, reach for more,
and remember my mother and father growing snow peas every season.
When she could hardly see anymore, my mother showed me
by feel how to plant 3 seeds per mound.
Every day, enough for dinner, and for leaving at neighbors' doors.
The birds surround me and eat and sing. I am unequivocally happy.

 —Maxine Hong Kingston

Maxine Hong Kingston was born in Stockton in 1940 and she came to Berkeley as a Cal freshman in 1958. After graduation she moved to Hawaii with her husband, Earll Kingston, an actor. In Hawaii she taught high school and wrote her first book, the best-selling breakthrough work in Asian American writing, *The Woman Warrior*, for which she received the National Book Critics Circle Award in nonfiction in 1976. *China Men* was published in 1980, followed by *Tripmaster Monkey* in 1989 and *The Fifth Book of Peace* in 2003. She returned to California and began teaching at Berkeley in 1990, and in 1994 Berkeley Repertory Theater produced a stage version of *The Woman Warrior,* as adapted by Deborah Rogin. In 2002 Kingston published a book of poems and reflections on writing poetry as an escape from the labor of prose, *To Be the Poet*, in which this poem appeared.

In my eyes he matches the gods, that man who
sits there facing you—any man whatever—
listening from closeby to the sweetness of your
      voice as you talk, the

sweetness of your laughter: yes, that—I swear it—
sets the heart to shaking inside my breast, since
once I look at you for a moment, I can't
      speak any longer,

but my tongue breaks down, and then all at once a
subtle fire races inside my skin, my
eyes can't see a thing and a whirring whistle
      thrums at my hearing,

cold sweat covers me and a trembling takes
ahold of me all over: I'm greener than the
grass is and appear to myself to be little
      short of dying.

But all must be endured, since even a poor....

    —Sappho, translated by Jim Powell

The record of European lyric poetry begins with **Sappho of Lesbos,** who lived toward the end of the seventh century BC on a Greek-speaking island off what is now the Turkish coast. Her work exists mostly as gorgeous and haunting fragments—bits of papyrus, pottery shards, quotations of lines from her songs in the work of later authors. This song, one of the few nearly complete ones to come down to us, survived because it was quoted by the philosopher Longinus in a treatise written in the first century AD, six hundred years or so after Sappho's death. Jim Powell, who studied classics and comparative literature at UC Berkeley, published this translation, echoing the original Greek meter, in his book *Sappho: A Garland* (1993).

THE CHILD ON THE SHORE

Wind, wind, give me back my feather
Sea, sea, give me back my ring
Death, death, give me back my mother
    So that she can hear me sing.

Song, song, go and tell my daughter
Tell her that I wear the ring
Say I fly upon the feather
    Fallen from the falcon's wing.

    —Ursula K. Le Guin

Ursula K. Le Guin was born in Berkeley in 1929 and grew up on Arch Street and in the Napa Valley. Her father, Alfred Kroeber, was one of the founders of the discipline of anthropology and one of the most distinguished scholars of his time. Her mother, Theodora, was the author of *The Inland Whale*, a classic book of California Indian stories, and *Ishi in Two Worlds*. Le Guin attended Radcliffe College, did graduate work in French literature at Columbia, and in 1953, on a ship to France to study, met her future husband, a young professor of history named Charles Le Guin. They were married that fall in Paris and eventually settled in Portland, where they had three children. Le Guin's first book, *Rocannon's World*, was published in 1966, and was followed by her classic trilogy for young adults, *A Wizard of Earthsea, The Tombs of Atuan,* and *The Farthest Shore,* which received the National Book Award in 1973 . Her novel *The Left Hand of Darkness* received Hugo and Nebula Awards and was followed by other classic works of fantasy and science fiction, including *The Word for World is Forest, The Dispossessed,* and *Always Coming Home,* one of several books set in a future northern California. Le Guin is also the author of several volumes of poems.

POSTSCRIPT

And some time make the time to drive out west
Into County Clare, along the Flaggy Shore,
In September or October, when the wind
And the light are working off each other
So that the ocean on one side is wild
With foam and glitter, and inland among stones
The surface of a slate-grey lake is lit
By the earthed lightning of a flock of swans,
Their feathers roughed and ruffling, white on white,
Their fully grown headstrong-looking heads
Tucked or cresting or busy underwater.
Useless to think you'll park and capture it
More thoroughly. You are neither here nor there,
A hurry through which known and strange things pass
As big soft buffetings come at the car sideways
And catch the heart off guard and blow it open.

   —Seamus Heaney

Known for his work as a poet, translator and critic **Seamus Heaney** was born on a farm outside of Belfast in Northern Ireland in 1939. He published his first books while living in Belfast in the 1960s, then spent an influential year in 1970 and 1971 in Berkeley as a visitor in the university's English department. He moved to the Irish Republic in 1972, where he has lived since then. He returned to Berkeley as a Beckman Professor in 1976, was a professor of poetry at Oxford from 1989 to 1994, and taught for many years at Harvard. In 1995 he was awarded the Nobel Prize for literature.

MENDOCINO MEMORY

for Haruko

Half moon
cold and low above the poplar tree
and sweet pea petals
pink and white/what
happened
on this personal best night
for casual stars
and silky constellations
streaming brilliant
through the far
forgetful darkness
of the sky

I found the other half
above the pillow
where you lay
asleep
face to one side
with nothing in this world
or the next
to hide

 —June Jordan

June Jordan (1936–2002) was born in Harlem and grew up in the Bedford-Stuyvesant neighborhood of Brooklyn. She attended Barnard and the University of Chicago, and began teaching at City College of New York in 1966. She taught at Sarah Lawrence and the State University of New York at Stony Brook and became a prolific author of political essays, poetry, children's books, and plays. She came to UC Berkeley in 1989 to teach African American studies and women's studies. In her decade at the university she was a political activist and an influential teacher, both of literature and of creative writing. Works from that time include a memoir, *Soldier: A Poet's Childhood;* two collections of essays, *Some of Us Did Not Die* and *Affirmative Acts;* and several books of poetry, among them *Kissing God Goodbye* and *Haruko/Love Poetry. June Jordan's Poetry for the People: A Revolutionary Blueprint,* for which Jordan wrote the introduction, is an account of the popular poetry-teaching and -learning program she initiated at the university.

The erosion of rocks blooms. The world
        that's for you thanks (you) actuality in actuality.
Large broad marks without interruption.
        Things as they fall in the hotel reduce
the view. This is in the world you all add up,
        the miniature terms of detail.
Sugar, two pigeons, a clean towel, the shadow
        —all add up to from the minute after after all.
The theater is less exciting. The erosion of rocks
        is a carnival for posterity
in its early stages. The theater suggests a house—
        a machine optimistic irritation. The world pretends
to get a fair distance on unshod horses. Using nails
        reduces the view. Things fall some of the way
out into the street, a new scene. A grid
        worn from one place to another. The erosion
of rocks washed away. The theater of holes dugs for trees.

    —Lyn Hejinian

Lyn Hejinian was born in the San Francisco Bay Area in 1941. She graduated from Harvard and in 1968 returned to California, where she met many of the young writers in Berkeley and San Francisco who were working in new and experimental forms. Soon she began to publish her own innovative poetry and prose, and her first book, *A Thought Is the Bride of What Thinking*, was published by Tuumba Press in 1976. In 1977 she married the jazz musician Larry Ochs. Her next book, *Writing Is an Aid to Memory*, appeared in 1978 from The Figures, and *Gesualdo* followed from Tuumba. The first of what would be several versions of her classic work of prose-poetry, *My Life* was published in 1980. Influential as an editor and essayist, she was one of the writers responsible for the revival of interest in Gertrude Stein in the 1980s, and she also served as president of the board of directors for Small Press Distribution. She taught at the California College of Arts and Crafts and at New College of California from 1986 to 1998. She joined the English department at UC Berkeley in 2001. Her later books include *The Cell, Oxota: A Short Russian Novel, The Cold of Poetry, A Border Comedy, Happily,* a collection of critical prose, *The Language of Inquiry,* and two volumes of translations of the Russian poet Arkadii Dragomoshchenko, *Description* and *Xenia.*

SONG

Afternoon cooking in the fall sun—
who is more naked
                            than the man
yelling, "Hey, I'm home!"
                to an empty house?
thinking because the bay is clear,
the hills in yellow heat,
& scrub oak red in gullies
        that great crowds of family
should tumble from the rooms
                    to throw their bodies on the Papa-body,
                            I-am-loved.

Cat sleeps in the windowgleam,
                dust motes.
        On the oak table
        filets of sole
stewing in the juice of tangerines,
        slices of green pepper
            on a bone-white dish.

    —Robert Hass

Robert Hass was born in San Francisco in 1941 and grew up in Marin County. He attended St. Mary's College and Stanford University. He lived in Berkeley while he was an undergraduate and moved back to the city in 1971. He taught at St. Mary's from 1971 until 1989, when he became a professor in the English department at UC Berkeley. His first book of poems, *Field Guide*, was published in 1973, and other books of prose and poetry followed, as well as translations of Japanese poetry and collaborative translations of the poetry of his friend Czeslaw Milosz. His three children attended Berkeley High. He served as poet laureate of the United States from 1995 to 1997.

ENCOUNTER

We were riding through frozen fields in a wagon at dawn.
A red wing rose in the darkness.

And suddenly a hare ran across the road.
One of us pointed to it with his hand.

That was long ago. Today neither of them is alive,
Not the hare, nor the man who made the gesture.

O my love, where are they, where are they going
The flash of a hand, streak of movement, rustle of pebbles.
I ask not out of sorrow, but in wonder.

—Czeslaw Milosz, translated by Lillian Vallee

Czeslaw Milosz (1911–2004) was born in Lithuania. Widely regarded as one of the great European poets of the twentieth century, he wrote some of his most memorable poems—published in Polish underground and resistance journals—during the Nazi occupation of Warsaw during World War II. He lived in France during the 1950s after renouncing his citizenship in protest against the Communist government of Poland, and he moved to Berkeley in 1960 when he was offered a job in the university's Slavic languages department. He lived with his family on Grizzly Peak in the Berkeley hills for almost forty years, writing poems that could not, until the collapse of the Communist Polish regime in 1989, be published in his own country. He received the Nobel Prize for literature in 1980. He died at his home in Krakow, where he had spent much of his final years, surrounded by the language in which he wrote and from which he had been exiled for almost fifty years.

KEEP ME

Keep me
From saying
Right now
In the ripeness of years:
Unharness the horses, Mikita,
I don't want to go
Anywhere.

Keep me
From saying
Such things.

—Malka Heifetz Tussman, translated by Kathryn Hellerstein

Malka Heifetz Tussman (1896–1987) was one of the best known and last surviving Yiddish poets. Born in the village of Bolshaya-Chaitcha in the southwest Ukraine, she immigrated to the United States with her family in 1912. She began to publish as early as 1919 in Yiddish journals in New York, Warsaw, and Toronto. Her first book of poems was published in 1949. Before moving to California, she attended the University of Wisconsin and taught in a Yiddish language school in Milwaukee. Later she moved to Los Angeles, where she was an elementary and high school teacher and an instructor at the University of Judaism. In 1971 she moved to Berkeley, where her son was a professor of philosophy, and she spent her last years here. In 1981 she received the Itsik Manger Prize for Poetry in Tel Aviv. Having outlived almost all her contemporaries, she was the last Yiddish-language poet to receive the award. Marcia Falk wrote a charming portrait of the elderly Heifetz Tussman in *With Teeth in the Earth: Selected Poems of Malka Heifetz Tussman*.

REASSURANCE

I must love the questions
themselves
as Rilke said
like locked rooms
full of treasure
to which my blind
and groping key
does not yet fit.

and await the answers
as unsealed
letters
mailed with dubious intent
and written in a very foreign
tongue.

and in the hourly making
of myself
no thought of Time
to force, to squeeze
the space
I grow into.

　　—Alice Walker

Alice Walker was born in Eatonton, Georgia, in 1944. She attended Spelman College in Atlanta, and, after traveling in Africa in 1964 and 1965, graduated from Sarah Lawrence, where she studied with Muriel Rukeyser, who helped her publish her first book of poetry, *Once*. From 1965 to 1978, she was engaged in the civil rights struggle in the South, worked for a Head Start program, married, gave birth to a daughter, and published a second book of poetry and two novels, *The Third Life of Grange Copeland* and *Meridian*. In 1978 she moved from Brooklyn to northern California. Her third novel, *The Color Purple*, received the Pulitzer Prize in 1983 and was followed by other books of fiction, essays, and poetry, including *The Temple of My Familiar, Possessing the Secret of Joy,* and *In Search of Our Mothers' Gardens*. During these years she has lived in Mendocino and Berkeley.

THE PANTHER

In the Jardin des Plantes, Paris

His vision, from the constantly passing bars,
has grown so weary that it cannot hold
anything else. It seems to him there are
a thousand bars; and behind the bars, no world.

As he paces in cramped circles, over and over,
the movement of his powerful soft strides
is like a ritual dance around a center
in which a mighty will stands paralyzed.

Only at times, the curtain of the pupils
lifts, quietly——. An image enters in,
rushes down through the tensed, arrested muscles,
plunges into the heart and is gone.

   —Rainer Maria Rilke, translated by Stephen Mitchell

Rainer Maria Rilke (1875–1926) is one of the great German-language poets of the twentieth century. He was born in Prague and lived in many parts of Europe, never permanently settling. In 1902 he moved to Paris to write a book on the sculptor Auguste Rodin, for whom he worked as secretary in 1905 and 1906. "The Panther," published in 1907, is one of Rilke's best-known works.

Stephen Mitchell was born in Brooklyn in 1943, attended Amherst and Yale, and came to Berkeley in 1977, where he lived until 2000. While doing graduate work in Hebrew studies, he met the Korean Zen teacher Seung Sahn, became a student of Zen, and edited a volume of Sahn's teachings, *Dropping Ashes on the Buddha*. He has published translations of the book of Job, of the poems of Rilke and the Chilean poet Pablo Neruda, and a version of the Chinese classic *Tao Te Ching* that became an unlikely best seller. His many books include *Parables and Portraits, Meetings with the Archangel,* and *The Gospel According to Jesus.*

AFTERNOON WALK: THE SEA RANCH

in memory of E.L.G.

Late light, uneven mole-gnawed meadow,
gullies, freshets, falls, whose start and speckle
Hopkins would have loved—and you—you too,
who loved the sheen and shade, the forest dapple
where grass meets cypress just beyond the house—
you'd praise the mushroom-sprout, the chilly glisten
as the hedgerow folds into the solstice
and suddenly the last crisp leaves unfasten.

This time of year, this place, light dims at the pace
of a long late walk—light seems to slow
and sorrow as the meadow turns its face
into your unlived season, the winter hollow
where only a steep sky, in quarter inches,
adjusts descending sun, ascending branches.

—Sandra M. Gilbert

Sandra M. Gilbert, a poet and influential feminist scholar, was born in New York City in 1936. She took a BA at Columbia, an MA at New York University, and a PhD at Cornell, and came to Berkeley in 1967, where she has lived for most of the last thirty-five years. She has taught at Sacramento State College, Hayward State College, and St. Mary's College, and as a visiting professor at the University of Indiana and Princeton. She has written many books of poetry, most recently *Kissing the Bread: New and Selected Poems 1969–1999* and *Belongings,* as well as a memoir, *Wrongful Death*, and a study of the poetry of D. H. Lawrence titled *Acts of Attention.* With Susan Gubar she is co-author of *The Madwoman in the Attic* and *No Man's Land* and co-editor of *The Norton Anthology of Literature by Women.* She is currently a professor of English at UC Davis. This poem remembers her husband, Elliot Gilbert, who was also a professor of English there.

THE WANT BONE

The tongue of the waves tolled in the earth's bell.
Blue rippled and soaked in the fire of blue.
The dried mouthbones of a shark in the hot swale
Gaped on nothing but sand on either side.

The bone tasted of nothing and smelled of nothing,
A scalded toothless harp, uncrushed, unstrung.
The joined arcs made the shape of birth and craving
And the welded-open shape kept mouthing O.

Ossified cords held the corners together
In groined spirals pleated like a summer dress.
But where was the limber grin, the gash of pleasure?
Infinitesimal mouths bore it away,

The beach scrubbed and etched and pickled it clean.
But O I love you it sings, my little my country
My food my parent my child I want you my own
My flower my fin my life my lightness my O.

—Robert Pinsky

Robert Pinsky was born in Long Branch, New Jersey, in 1940 and attended Rutgers and Stanford. He came to UC Berkeley in the early 1980s as a professor of English and lived on Monterey Avenue. Two of his daughters graduated from Berkeley High. His many Berkeley writer friends included Thom Gunn, Robert Hass, Brenda Hillman, Tom Farber, Wendy Lesser, Leonard Michaels, Alan Williamson, Czeslaw Milosz, and Stephen Mitchell. Pinsky was for a decade an influential teacher of young poets and he published during his Berkeley years *History of My Heart, Poetry and the World,* and *The Want Bone,* and collaborated with Robert Hass and Czeslaw Milosz on a translation of Milosz's *The Separate Notebooks.* In 1990 he returned to the East Coast and took a position at Boston University. He served as poet laureate of the United States from 1997 to 2000.

SIV, WITH OCEAN (PACIFIC)

Lace woven and rewoven with every wave
and then let slip from her shoulder to reveal,
only to conceal again. Cliffs marching off
into the mist in the distance. Into this moment
the redwoods have flung themselves, out of the green
tangle below the terrace, up past our vision,
chunky and vast and thronging with bluejays and
ravens that dart out of their darknesses to
forage among the plates of the people lunching
there— up into the blue sky that goes all the way
to the horizon. Past her profile you can just make out
a bit of the road that runs north and south behind her,
out of view. Far out, on the various blues, all of them
moving, the wakes of the little boats intersect each other
and fade in the foam, lace woven and rewoven. She
and the moment are one thing, contained, the way the shoulder
of that cliff is just slipping back into the mist, the way
the various blues, all of them moving, are marching off
toward the horizon

   —Ron Loewinsohn

Ron Loewinsohn was born in the Philippines in 1937 and came to the United States with his family in 1945. He went to high school in San Francisco, where, wandering in North Beach, he met most of the writers who made the city a literary capital—Allen Ginsberg, Robert Duncan, Jack Spicer, and Richard Brautigan. He spent afternoons reading poetry in the upstairs loft at City Lights Bookstore, wrote poems, and supported himself as a printer. He began attending the UC Berkeley in 1965, finished in 1967, did graduate work at Harvard, and returned to join Berkeley's English faculty in 1970. He is the author of many books of poetry and two novels, including *Magnetic Field(s),* which won the Bay Area Book Reviewers Award for fiction in 1983.

FOR JACK SPICER

I'm out of touch with stars. The bar's
closed. We go groggy down Grant
to Columbus to the Park to somebody's parked car.
One of us says, Let's go to Ebbe's. Ebbe says,
Sure, why not, let's go. We're gone
piled in the back seat breathing wine on windowpanes.
Seven Years ago. Tonight

you're gone. Maybe that night it was
Marco who fell back on the bush.
We left him there to sleep it off.

    —David Meltzer

David Meltzer was born in Rochester, New York, in 1937. His father, a cellist, also wrote comedy for radio and television. Meltzer grew up in Brooklyn, where he was a child singer on the radio and early television. He moved to Los Angeles with his father and attended Los Angeles City College and UCLA, but he dropped out and chose instead to take artists and poets as mentors and guides. He came to San Francisco in 1957 and began reading his poetry to jazz accompaniment at the Jazz Cellar in North Beach. From 1961 to 1970 he worked at the Discovery Bookstore in North Beach. During those years he edited *The Journal for the Protection of All Beings* with Michael McClure, Lawrence Ferlinghetti, and Gary Snyder, and performed with his wife, Tina, in Berkeley and North Beach folk clubs. Between 1968 and 1970 he also wrote ten agit-porn novels for the North Hollywood publisher Essex House. He has taught at the Urban School and San Francisco State New College, and he developed a creative writing program at Vacaville prison. He edited *The San Francisco Poets* in 1971 and two anthologies—*Birth* and *Death*—for Jack Shoemaker's North Point Press. *Arrows: Selected Poetry 1957–1992* was published in 1995. Recent publications include *San Francisco Beat: Talking with the Poets* and *Beat Thing. David's Copy,* a selected poetry collection, will be published in 2005 by Viking Penguin. Meltzer lives in Oakland.

from **IT'S GO IN**
      QUIET ILLUMINED GRASS
                  LAND

silver half freezing in day
                        elation the
                        outside
of the outside sky walking
                        rose

silver half freezing in day
                        moon's elation
of the outside rose, his seeing
                        on both
                        'sides'
seeing someone else at all and the
                        half freezing
elation of the outside so that's even
                        with one
continually over and over one / person

    —Leslie Scalapino

Leslie Scalapino was born in Santa Barbara, California, and raised in Berkeley, where she attended John Muir Elementary, Willard Junior High, and Berkeley High School. She later graduated from Reed College and attended graduate school at UC Berkeley. She has written many books of innovative poetry, fiction, and essays. Her first two books, *O and Other Poems* and *The Woman Who Could Read the Minds of Dogs*, were published by Sand Dollar Books, a press run out of Jack and Vicki Shoemaker's Sand Dollar Bookstore on Solano Avenue. Among her other books are *Considering How Exaggerated Music Is, That They Were at the Beach,* and *Way*—all published by North Point Press in Berkeley—as well as *Defoe, New Time, It's Go In/Quiet Illumined Grass/Land,* and a trilogy, *The Return of Painting, The Pearl,* and *Orion.*

HERMETIC SONG, IV

for Robert Duncan

There were nine grand pianos in my father's house
one a water object in my head
and one a ship of glass

one an eye on the end of a branch
and one a paint-pot spilling red
There were live fandangos in the father's house

so that sleepers might sleep within the dance
and set their images to rest
Please tell me if you can

Did it snow pure snow in some father's house
and did the children chant Whether me this
then Whether me that

There was a winding stair in this father's house
climbing or falling no one would say
There were notebooks and nightbooks

and voices enclosed by a ring of bone
They were crying Wait Don't Wait
There were travelers standing at the gate

 —Michael Palmer

Michael Palmer was born in New York City in 1943. He attended Harvard, majored in French, and took a master's degree in comparative literature. He married the architect Cathy Simon and moved to San Francisco in 1972, where he has lived for thirty years in Noe Valley. His early books, *Blake's Newton, The Circular Gates,* and *Without Music,* were published by Black Sparrow Press in the 1970s and another three, *Notes for Echo Lake, First Figure,* and *Sun,* were published by Berkeley's North Point Press in the 1980s. From 1975 to 1984 Palmer was poet-in-residence with the Margaret Jenkins Dance Company, which produced many collaborative works fusing poetry and dance. He has been a Holloway Lecturer in the Practice of Poetry at UC Berkeley and taught at St. Mary's College and New College of California. His selected poems, *The Lion Bridge*, was published in 1998. He has also published two volumes of translations of the French poet Emmanuel Hocquard.

- - -   - - -

LEFT EYE

There's a barrier before between

I think they were trying to write their names on it

The rubbed-looking light   a glare of the all along
Had inserted itself into the nerves' lining

Say you saw it   Be alive

As if comprehension were not to blame

As if autonomy were not to blame

And to the you between us   there could be read
          (a   heap of dirt had been pushed up, outside)

In the numberless

Rumorless

Night   the flame narrative   the flame report

+ + +   + + +

   —Brenda Hillman

124

Brenda Hillman was born in 1951 in Tucson, Arizona, and grew up there. She also lived in Brazil, where her mother was born. After attending Pomona College and the University of Iowa Writers' Workshop, she came to Berkeley in 1973, married the writer and university professor Leonard Michaels, and worked at University Press Books. She raised three children in the 1980s and 90s and produced a steady flow of books of original poetry, including *White Dress, Fortress, Bright Existence, Death Tractates, Loose Sugar,* and *Cascadia,* all from Wesleyan University Press. She also published several chapbooks, including *Autumn Sojourn* and *The Firecage.* She has been a Holloway Lecturer at UC Berkeley and she teaches in the graduate writing program at St. Mary's College. She married the poet Robert Hass in 1995, and she currently lives in Kensington.

POSITIONS OF THE BODY, VIII

               You had wanted to go back, to step
back in time, through art: before *Guernica;*
The Raft of the Medusa; Executions of 3rd May, 1808;
before the weight of Christ's body,
failing the rigid geometry of the cross,
documented suffering.
               You stood
in the duecento, expecting icon only—the body
abstracted, formal, schematic—and Giotto
had chosen a greenish cast for the skin,

straining the upheld arms, skewing
the wounded torso and bent legs, bowing forward
the still face: Word made flesh, not stylized; dead
weight to be lifted down, angels writhing.

So the exhumation of murdered nuns

in El Salvador, priests and cameras
called to the makeshift grave (you had watched
in tarnished light): how the bodies

               were awkwardly moved
(your hands clasped tightly together),
how they tangled and did not cover themselves.

   —Carol Snow

Carol Snow was born in San Francisco in 1949 and grew up within shouting distance of the zoo and Ocean Beach. She attended Berkeley for two years as an undergraduate in the experimental Tussman Program (founded by philosophy professor Joseph Tussman, the son of Yiddish poet Malka Heifetz Tussman) and stayed on in Berkeley in an apartment near the Rose Garden, where she says she tried to write songs and, "having run out of chord changes," turned to lyric alone. She has been a San Francisco resident since the late 1970s and is co-director of the Blue Bear School of Music. Her books of poetry include *Artist and Model, For,* and *The Seventy Prepositions.* She was a Holloway Lecturer in Poetry at UC Berkeley in 2002.

JUDY COMES TO VISIT

Judy asks, "You
don't have those
wrinkles on the back
of your neck, do you?"
Alarmed, I ask,
"What wrinkles?"
Scott slaps the table.
"Give us a *break*!
Don't give her
something new
to worry about!"

The next day, he
catches me staring
at my wrinkles. He
grabs my hand &
stomps out, pulling
me along. "STOP
this crap!" he shouts.
"Work on your spiritual
development!"

   —Alta

Alta was born in Reno, Nevada, in 1942, and in 1954 her family moved to Berkeley so her brother could attend the Berkeley School for the Blind. She attended UC Berkeley from 1965 to 1967, began to write poetry, and learned with her then-husband John Oliver Simon to use a printing press. In 1969 she founded Shameless Hussy Press and began to publish fiction and poetry by women emerging from the burgeoning feminist movement, including work by Judy Grahn and Ntozake Shange. Her own works include *Letters to Women; Burn This and Memorize Yourself; Song of the Wife, Song of the Mistress; No Visible Means of Support;* and *I Am Not a Practicing Angel.* In 1980 Judy Grahn edited a selection of her work, *The Shameless Hussy: Selected Stories, Essays, and Poetry.* When it closed in 1989, Shameless Hussy had published more than fifty volumes of women's writing.

MORNING *MINYAN*

A quorum of small black birds
has settled on the tree outside my window:
ten of them, enough to pray
the most sacred prayers.
Whom do they beseech,
for what do they pray
with their *too-toos* and *dee-dee-dees*?
Do they ask for grace?
Cannot be. They already have it.
Do they seek forgiveness? For what?
They cannot help but do what birds do.
Do they need healing?
Perhaps one of them has broken a wing?
Or are they singing the praises of the Creator?
Of the creation?
Of the many ilks and varieties of birds?

I would like to stay and find out
but I have no time this morning.
No time no time no time no time chants my species.

Dit-dit-dit, dit-dit-dit, dit-dit-dit-dit
cry the birds as they fly away.

  —Marcia Falk

Marcia Falk was born and raised in the metropolitan New York area, where she studied painting at the Art Students League. She received a BA in philosophy from Brandeis and a PhD in comparative literature from Stanford, and was a postdoctoral fellow in Hebrew literature at the Hebrew University of Jerusalem. She has two books of poems, *This Year in Jerusalem* and *It Is July in Virginia*, and two books of translations from Hebrew, *The Spectacular Difference: Selected Poems of Zelda* and *The Song of Songs: Love Lyrics from the Bible*, which will be reissued in a new edition in fall of 2004. She has also published a volume of translations from Yiddish, *With Teeth in the Earth: Selected Poems of Malka Heifetz Tussman*. She met Tussman in the spring of 1973 when they read together at a Jewish arts festival in Berkeley; that summer Falk rented a room in Berkeley and met with Tussman daily to translate poems. Falk taught English and Hebrew literature and creative writing at the State University of New York, Binghamton, and the Claremont Colleges before returning to live in Berkeley in 1988. In 1996 she published *The Book of Blessings,* a re-creation of Jewish prayer in Hebrew and English poetic forms. She has recently returned to painting, her first love.

5. DETROIT ANNIE, HITCHHIKING *from* THE COMMON WOMAN

Her words pour out as if her throat were a broken
artery and her mind were cut-glass, carelessly handled.
You imagine her in a huge velvet hat with great
dangling black feathers,
but she shaves her head instead
and goes for three-day midnight walks.
Sometimes she goes down to the dock and dances
off the end of it simply to prove her belief
that people who cannot walk on water
are phonies, or dead.
When she is cruel, she is very, very
cool and when she is kind she is lavish.
Fisherman think perhaps she's a fish, but they're all
fools. She figured out that the only way
to keep from being frozen was to
stay in motion, and long ago converted
most of her flesh into liquid. Now when she
smells danger, she spills herself all over,
like gasoline, and lights it.
She leaves the taste of salt and iron
Under your tongue, but you don't mind.
The common woman is as common
As the reddest wine.

   —Judy Grahn

Judy Grahn was born in Chicago in 1940 and raised in New Mexico. After being dismissed from the U.S. Air Force for being a lesbian, she attended Howard University in Washington, D.C., from 1963 to 1966 and then moved to the Bay Area, where she founded the Oakland Women's Press Collective. Her first book, *Edward the Dyke and Other Poems,* was published in 1971. It was followed in 1973 by *The Common Woman,* from which this poem comes, and *A Woman Is Talking to Death* in 1974. Grahn eventually returned to school at San Francisco State and received a BA in 1984. During that time she established a gay and lesbian studies program at New College of San Francisco. Her later books include *The Queen of Wands* and *The Queen of Swords.* She lives in Oakland.

COTTON IN A PILL BOTTLE

I love the fog. It's not one hundred degrees.
It's not Mary sobbing on the phone or powder-
white mildew killing the rose. My father
lost inside it keeps pretending he's dead
just so he can get a little peace.
It's not made of fire or afraid of fire
like me, it has nothing to do with smoke.
There's never any ash, anything to sift through.
You just put your hand on the yellow rail
and the steps seem to move themselves.
It doesn't have a job to do.
It's morning all afternoon.
It loves the music but would be
just as happy listening to the game.
Still, I don't know what frightens me.
It doesn't blame anyone.
You'll never see tears on its cheeks.
It'll never put up a fight.
I love how the fog lies down in the air,
how it can get only so far from the sea.

  —Dean Young

Dean Young was born in Pennsylvania in 1955. Married to the novelist Cornelia Nixon, a UC Berkeley graduate, he began spending summers in Berkeley in 1983 before moving there permanently in 1992. He teaches half of each year at the Iowa Writers' Workshop. Young is the author of *Design with X, Beloved Infidel, Strike Anywhere, First Course in Turbulence,* and *Skid.* In this poem we find him trying to come to terms with the Berkeley weather.

THREE HAIKU

What voice,
what song, spider,
   in the autumn wind?

                    —Bashō

   *

The spring sea rising
and falling, rising
   and falling all day.

                    —Buson

   *

Even with insects—
some can sing,
   some can't.

                    —Issa

—translated by Robert Hass

Matsuo Bashō (1644–1694), **Yosa Buson** (1716–1784), and **Kobayashi Issa** (1763–1827) are three of the most important poets in the Japanese haiku tradition. Bashō was its originator, a poet of great spiritual intensity. Buson was a painter as well as a poet, and a sharp observer of the physical world. Issa, the son of a mountain farmer, often wrote humorous poems. These translations come from Robert Hass's *The Essential Haiku: Versions of Bashō, Buson, and Issa,* work he did in the 1970s and 80s. It belongs—with Witter Bynner's and Kiang Kang-hu's *The Jade Mountain,* Kenneth Rexroth's *One Hundred Poems from the Japanese* and *One Hundred Poems from the Chinese,* Gary Snyder's *Cold Mountain Poems,* and Mill Valley poet Jane Hirshfield's *The Ink Dark Moon*—to a tradition of interest in classical Asian poetry among Bay Area poets. Even Czeslaw Milosz, from his study on Grizzly Peak, produced translations of haiku into Polish.

ARRIVAL

We've come to the place
and stepped down. Once again
it's our footsteps on the porch.
We've put away our toys.
Ahead the port, the restaurant
and bar. We pass the chessplayers
in the park and the old dressed in black
dozing on benches. In the law court
we take a seat by the door
and look up at the balcony.
We visit city hall. Or we march
in reviews and wave flags.
We pick apples, or berries.
Or we build castles on the beach,
taking care with the moats
and turrets. There's the ice cream truck.
We eat lunch at noon in the square
and children wade in the fountain. So much
traffic! Bells ring on the playground
or in the steeple. Tourists hold up maps
and we give directions.

—Patricia Dienstfrey

Patricia Dienstfrey was born in Montreal, Canada, in 1939 and grew up in New England. She was educated at Radcliffe and came to Berkeley in 1962 to attend graduate school in city planning, after which she married, had three children, and began writing poetry. In meetings of the Berkeley Poets' Co-op in the early 1970s, she met five other women—Laura Moriarity, Karen Brodine, Marina La Palma, Kit Duane, and Rena Rosenwasser—with whom she founded Kelsey Street Press in 1974 to bring out original work by women writers. Among her books of poetry are *Newspaper Stories and Other Poems, Small Salvations, The Woman Without Experiences,* and *Love and Illustration.* With Brenda Hillman, whom she met at University Press Books, where they both worked in the 1970s, she edited *The Grand Permission: New Writings on Poetics and Motherhood.* She lives in Berkeley with her husband, Ted, a city planner.

from **INK**

Glimmer of light high over Mount Diablo (silhouette flat across the hot hazy day) would be an airplane. Each truck is a roving sign for the products within. A loose blouse barely buttoned. Influence governs chains of the imaginable. She speaks and the illusion is shattered: she's a reactionary (to which you respond by nodding before moving down the bar). The original lyrics were *tuti fruti, good booty.* Butch gal on her own chopped Harley. I ride the bus. Roofing gang, on a break, crowds into the orange donut shop. More "private" cops than real ones in America today. She uses one crutch as a sort of cane. Next to three Latino youths, each wearing a baseball cap with the bill turned back, catcher-style. O lord, raspberry vanilla ice cream. Old guy, riding the bus for the sake of it. He's 400 lbs. of soft flesh, pink almost, and, even though he's balding, the eyes and mouth of an infant. The driver hops out of the bus and into the corner market for a styrofoam cup of coffee and, while waiting (a tall light-skinned black man with a muscular build, short afro almost red), he relaxes, lets go for a second of that tension, that needing to be in control of his crowd of rowdy passengers as well as the traffic, and his whole body changes, shifts, shoulders slump suddenly rounded, spine curves, until he's a smaller man, no longer young at all. Chances as at slathering.

—Ron Silliman

Ron Silliman's family has been living in the East Bay since the late nineteenth century. One of his grandmothers was born near what is now the West Oakland BART train station in 1897 and grew up in Berkeley. She met her husband, the poet's grandfather, in the playground at LeConte School during the fifth grade. Ron was born in 1946 and began writing poetry while "hanging out among the street people of Telegraph Avenue" in 1964 and 65. With Bob Grenier, whom he met while a student at UC Berkeley, and Barret Watten, Lyn Hejinian, and Carla Harryman, he became a founding presence in a literary group that came to be known as the "language poets," who were interested in abstract and formally experimental uses of language. In imitation of abstract impressionist painters, they were concerned not so much with saying something with language but in doing something with it as a material. Among Silliman's projects was *BART,* which depicts "a journey on the entire transit system taken on Labor Day 1976 in a single run-on sentence." Always political, Silliman hosted a radio program about prison movement organizing on Pacifica Radio in the 1970s and he edited *The Socialist Review* from offices near Adeline and Ashby. He moved to Pennsylvania in 1995 with his wife and two sons, and he currently works in the computer industry while remaining active as a poet, editor, and literary critic.

RESERVATION

By the collision of different sentiments, sparks of truth are set out,
and political light is obtained.
    —Benjamin Franklin

Birth, by analogy, is a counterexample to
invention: Suddenly you face a new tune
highly sensitive to its *own* meter and
material. (I was born with a bandit's
nose in my ear and two lightning
rods in either hand that Art had
ambiguously arranged. Everything was neatly poised to
fill my mouth with the speaking things
of the world.) Things of the world!
Things of the world! An "American Electricity"
laps up miles of motion, leaping from
body to sun, a most violent intervention
on a night of the ingenious self.
These arousements have landed us where single
shots and tangled showers devolve upon the
tongue as it explains forward the flourishing
morning grass, where rain couldn't fall on
you, and in the evening we might
mow the borderless land—borderless ourselves and
home at last in our own right minds.

    —Jean Day

Jean Day was born in Syracuse, New York, in 1954, but her family had deep ties to the Bay Area. Her grandmother graduated from UC Berkeley, where she was a friend of the poet Genevieve Taggard, and her grandfather was rector of All Soul's Church on Cedar Street. In a nearby house their daughter, Day's mother, survived the catastrophic 1923 Berkeley fire. Day arrived in San Francisco in 1976, fresh out of Antioch College in Ohio, and started working at Small Press Distribution, which was then called Serendipity Books Distribution and operated out of a tiny warehouse behind Peter Howard's Serendipity Books on Shattuck Avenue. In 1979 she moved from San Francisco to Berkeley and lived in a tiny studio—"more like a cupboard"—in a house on LaVereda that was built by a Danish sea captain. Among her books of poetry are *The I and the You, The Literal World,* and *Enthusiasm.* She currently works for UC Berkeley, where she is managing editor of the academic journal *Representations.*

THE BEAUTIFUL HOUSE

Mice wizards baskets bells
"Maze" where the object is to be
At the same place as yourself
At the same time

Wedding invitations vase delphinium
Books taxes recipes cases
"Netherworld," the game of senet
Where stick are thrown like
Bones your try to get through

The day and then the day
Quick but careful, plain
Full dripping camellias
Breathless waking or deep
Sleep full of air achingly
Blue starred egg painted
World opening to another.
Names like letters
Entwined hieroglyphs: us

Columbine a dove, flower or
Love of Harlequin. Mine is air and yours
The right time. The last move.
The beautiful house.

   —Laura Moriarty

Laura Moriarty was born in St. Paul, Minnesota, in 1952 and raised in Massachusetts and California. She attended UC Berkeley in the 1970s and she designed for herself an individual major in the practice of poetry. An early member of the Berkeley Poets' Co-op, she has played an active part in the thriving Bay Area experimental poetry scene and was a founding member of Kelsey Street Press. She published her own work with other local presses printing experimental writing, including Avec, O Books, Krupskaya, and Post Apollo. She has worked at the Poetry Center at San Francisco State University and now works for Small Press Distribution, the Berkeley-based company that promotes the national distribution books from small and experimental presses. She lives in Albany.

from **PROPERTY**

*The rowboat was caught in the mudflats. A few gulls padded around
it. The mud fizzled. A grey mist was broken by a narrow sky. In the
distance a solitary cathedral interfered with the sensuality of
endlessness. The earth was small and even cosy, until, looking up at
the beaming monstrosity, one recognized the meagerness of its
claim on space.*

—Carla Harryman

Carla Harryman was born in Orange County in 1952. She received a BA from UC Berkeley in 1975 and an MA from San Francisco State, directed the American Poetry Archive at San Francisco State's Poetry Center from 1978 to 1982, and worked for the University Art Museum from 1982 to 1987. Married to the poet Barrett Watten, she is associated with the group of experimental poets in Berkeley and San Francisco in the 1970s and 80s who worked on what has been described as language-centered writing. Harryman's work mixes the textures of prose narrative, poetry, drama, and the essay. Her play *Memory Play* was first produced in 1994. Her other works include *Percentage, There Never Was a Rose Without a Thorn,* and *The Words*.

ROOM *from* HOW TO IMPROVE

for Barrett Watten

Writing is a room, a method of dilating the pupils. Horace speaks: "Listen. I have a surface. Every day, at least. Then I sentence words to various shades of meaning. Day after day I am looking at that picked garden. Amaranthine glory of her leonine dignity sat gravely on the gypsying hinterlands."

You can verify your so-and-so. You can merely know how to use it. Let it go at that. We can stop. We haven't learned at all, technical, specialized. Equal in value with the royal background.

> I might have known.
> The immaculate pencil.
> The inexcusable, comma.
> Ritual lives of endless objects.

Define your own scorn. Redden, endless, extravagant. Couch upon the bed, lake, beast. Look at what you can. Try to avoid preceding today. Follow splendor about. It does shine figuratively with a magnificence firmly between its teeth.

—Bob Perelman

Bob Perelman was born in Ohio in 1947. He and his wife, the painter Francie Shaw, moved to the Bay Area in 1976, where he was active in the Bay Area language poetry scene (along with Ron Silliman, Lyn Hejinian, and Barrett Watten) and helped organize a series of influential evenings of talk about poetry and poetics at the San Francisco arts venue 80 Langton Street. He edited two volumes of these talks under the titles *Hills Talks* and *Writing/Talks*. A critic as well as a poet, he earned a doctorate in English at UC Berkeley and left the Bay Area in 1990 to become a professor at the University of Pennsylvania. His books of poems include *Ten to One: Selected Poems, The Future of Memory,* and a painting/poetry collaboration with his wife, *Playing Bodies*. His books of criticism include *The Trouble with Genius* and *The Marginalization of Poetry*.

from **REAL ESTATE, IV**

Doubt compares with everything: in pure air the constant ringing of a distant alarm. The magnetic needle links up to remembered North in a bipolar manner. The exercise yard refuses to yield: a mid-Oakland freeway stack marks a drop in potential. The battle of fixtures stabilizes at a determinate point: vertigo is aware of inscriptions (territory melts down in time). Neutral fillers make a hole in one's life: the lights go on, the suction pump prepares a seduction. Furnished apartments decorate the cube of the state: the slag heap is backed up by polished metal engines. Parallel avenues converge on a syntax having no center of its own: a motionless drill restores the site to crash landings. The increments multiply in the absence of scale: the landscape retreats to vague promises of suspension. A tour of Mt. Erebus is conveyed to the equitorial plane: the camera releases energy into the world it dismantles. A vaporized world built of airtight containers (the size of the prison) and cryptic flux (the time spent therein). But the job of the driver is to muffle the sound of the new car turning into parts. To perfect the extraction of data from what's not event: the "sign-off" radiates from the end of the broadcast. All this gets us nowhere: the cloud arrives at ground zero, ready to stop at once.

—Barrett Watten

Barrett Watten was born in Long Beach, California, in 1948 and spent his childhood in California, Japan, and Taiwan. After graduating from high school in Oakland, he attended MIT and then UC Berkeley, where he took a degree in science, met Robert Grenier and Ron Silliman, and studied with Josephine Miles. He attended the Iowa Writers' Workshop from 1970 to 1972 and then returned to the Bay Area and became active in the group of experimental writers known as language poets. He edited the magazine *This* and co-edited *Poetics Journal*. In the mid-1980s he moved back to Berkeley, where he lived on Stuart and McGee Streets and worked as an editor of the academic journal *Representations* while he pursued a PhD in English. His books include *Opera—Works, Decay, 1-10, Conduit, Under Erasure,* and *Bad History.* He has also written a number of critical works, including *Total Syntax* in 1984, which became a manifesto of the language poetry movement. Married to the writer Carla Harryman, he is currently a professor of English at Wayne State University in Detroit.

from **MIND OVER MATTER**

Only two know the meaning of us
And even they can't be trusted
This critique infers a doomed finesse
I am here to remind you that time
Has its own blind market forces
Poetry is not exempt
Who uses it creates a small scandal
As real as thinking
Perfectly sharp yet entirely vague
What thou lov'st well is thy true heritage
This shattered beauty holding up the world bank
Poetry loves with love
The *bon mot* knows no hate
That's what we meant in 1968

   —Gloria Frym

Gloria Frym was born in Brooklyn in 1947, grew up in Los Angeles, and lived for some years in New Mexico. She arrived in Berkeley in 1976 "in a Volkswagen and a tie-dyed t-shirt" and threw herself into the Bay Area poetry world. Her first book of poems, *Impossible Affection,* was published in 1979. She also published that year *Second Stories: Interviews with Women Artists,* took a job at the university's art museum, and set out to make a living as an art critic, but found, she said, that she "couldn't write fast enough." She taught poetry at San Francisco State and in the San Francisco County jails. From 1987 to 2002 she was on the faculty of the Poetics Program at New College of San Francisco, and she now teaches at the California College of Arts and Crafts. Her work consists of several books of poetry—including *Back to Forth, By Ear,* and *Homeless at Home,* which won a 2002 American Book Award—and two books of stories, *How I Learned* and *Distance No Object.*

I DANCED WITH YOU ONCE ONLY ONLIEST ONE

the extended malady of your metaphor has finally reached me
across these seas of light ... unabashed I gaze at that reduction
you are in your swimming suit ready to eternalize your form
on celluloid ... if death has a beginning does it also have an end?
such interrogations on Saint Nothing Day! the jazz is full of dis-
sonance smoke the raucous cries of the illiterate suffering of the shoulder
like a musk-ox buried in eons of ice ... your shadow in its violent context
nothing about this bores me ... I have to read the entire passage
possessed by lunacy of the muse and her subjective total cigarette
the way your hair covered your eyes like night and absence
the how-do-you-do of undiscovered sexual impulses irritating
when you want to really consider the categorical imperative
... and they open the window on the unwritten epic... intuitive-
ly supposing the gunwale and the spear have some unconscious connection
....it was dancing in the snow
to your premature configuration of excoriated angels
shibboleth of infancy on the dirt-farm where they put father to work
a regard for the less delicate emotions raped with a shovel crosswise
I make no distinctions between the genders and sleep vertically
in the nimbus of the water of the shadow of the hopeless Persephone
and after so many years can still reconstruct the map to your house
as if lifted on sandstone cliffs above the breath of time
... in an automobile half-frozen in the back seat witnessing decay

—Ivan Arguelles

Ivan Arguelles was born in Rochester, Minnesota, in 1939. He was raised in Mexico City, Los Angeles, and Rochester, and took a degree in classics at the University of Chicago. He arrived in Berkeley in 1978, went to work as a librarian at the university, and made friends with other writers, including Jack Foley, Andrew Joron, and the chronicler of the Beat generation Neeli Cherkovski. He came to surrealism through books, first reading the New York poets Frank O'Hara and John Ashbery, and then turning to the Spanish, to Federico Garcia Lorca and the great Peruvian poet César Vallejo. He also met the already legendary San Francisco surrealist Philip Lamantia when he arrived in the Bay Area. Arguelles developed his style, he has said, "working with the muse in the pizza dives south of campus." He co-founded Pantograph Press in 1992 and his books include *The Invention of Spain, "That" Goddess, Hapax Legomenon, Looking for Mary Lou* (which won the William Carlos Williams Award of the Poetry Society of America), the two-volume *Madonna Septet,* and *Triloka.*

ICE CUBE

you're
good
at
conversation

it's
like
walking
you

put
one
word
in

front
of
the
other

—Kit Robinson

Kit Robinson was born in Evanston, Illinois, in 1949, attended high school in Cincinnati, and graduated from Yale in 1971. When he arrived shortly thereafter in San Francisco, he worked as a cab driver, teacher's aide, postal clerk, court reporter, and legal proofreader. An early member of the language poets circle, he also directed the San Francisco California Poets in the Schools program from 1976 to 1983, the Tenderloin Writers Workshop, and the NewLangstonArts literature program. With Lyn Hejinian he founded "In the American Tree: New Writing by Poets," a weekly radio program of live readings and interviews on the Berkeley station KPFA. His play, *Collateral,* was produced by Poets Theater in San Francisco in 1982. His books, including *The Crave, Balance Sheet,* and *Windows,* have been published by many of the experimental small presses that sprang up in Berkeley and the Bay Area in the 1980s and 90s: Atelos, Chax, Potes & Poets, Post Apollo, Roof, The Figures, This, Tuumba, Whale Cloth, and Zasterle. He has lived in Berkeley since 1982 with his partner, Ahni, and since 1983 has been employed in the information technology industry.

```
                                        s  s
                                        o  t            W
                           b            y  r    w       e
                  s    t   u            a  i    e
                  n i  h   r            b  n    r
                  o n  e   i            e  g    e
                  w m  e   d            a  i
                           d            n  n
                                        s  g


              gninrom  txen  gnidnif

      drah  saw  dloc  saw      otni  etib


         We  opened  our  mouths  onebyone

                    snowflakes
```

```
M
O
R
C
E
L
S

b
e
t
w
e
e
n
t
h
e
l
i
n
e
s
```

```
a            
w    w       
a    a       
k    s    n  
e         o  
          o  
          n  
          e  
```

—Theresa Hak Kyung Cha

Theresa Hak Kyung Cha (1951–1982) was born in Pusan, Korea, and with her family immigrated to the United States when she was thirteen. They spent a year in Hawaii and arrived in the Bay Area in 1964. She received a BA in comparative literature from UC Berkeley in 1973 and an MFA in art practice in 1978. In 1976 she did postgraduate work in filmmaking in Paris and studied film theory with the renowned scholar Christian Metz. A filmmaker, visual artist, and writer, she blurred the boundaries of these genres in her work. Her films include *Passages Paysages* and *Exilée,* which showed at the San Francisco Art Institute and the Museum of Modern Art in San Francisco. In 1982 she married the photographer Richard Barnes and moved to New York. She was murdered there in November 1982, the year in which her best-known work, *Dictée,* was published.

SOUTH SIDE *of* **ADDISON STREET,**
from **SHATTUCK** *to* **MILVIA**

Hey, fog, go home.
Go home, fog.
Pelican is beating your wife.

*

I dream of you.
I dream of you jumping,
rabbit, jackrabbit, quail.

—Ohlone songs

These songs were gathered by Alfred Kroeber of the UC Berkeley anthropology department in Monterey in 1901. His informants were Maria Viviana Soto, who was then seventy-eight years old, and her niece, Jacinta Gonzales. Soto was born in 1823, the year in which the mission system collapsed. Her father, Salvador Morciegano—his native name was Mucjay—was born in Big Sur in 1796, just before the arrival of Europeans on that stretch of coast. Like most of the Ohlones of northern California, he was drawn, or pressed, into the mission system. What is known of him is that he was baptized at the Mission Carmel in 1807. The songs Maria Soto and her niece sang to Professor Kroeber in Monterey were an echo of an earlier time and a still-intact native culture. Kroeber returned to Monterey in April and asked the women to sing the songs into his recording instruments. The wax cylinders on which these songs were recorded are in the university's Phoebe A. Hearst Museum of Anthropology. Both women died in Monterey in the influenza epidemic of 1916–17.

from VERSES ON THE PROSPECT OF PLANTING ARTS AND LEARNING IN THE NEW WORLD

In happy climes, the seat of innocence,
    Where nature guides and virtue rules,
Where men shall not impose for truth or sense
    The pedantry of courts and schools:

There shall be sung another golden age,
    The rise of empire and of arts,
The good and great inspiring epic rage,
    The wisest heads and noblest hearts.

Not such as Europe breeds in her decay;
    Such as she bred when fresh and young,
When heavenly fame did animate her clay,
    By future poets shall be sung.

Westward the course of empire takes its way;
    The first four acts already past,
A fifth shall close the drama with the day;
    Time's noblest offspring is the last.

—Bishop George Berkeley

This is the poem that gave the city of Berkeley its name. It was written in 1752 by **George Berkeley** (1685–1753), an Irish-born philosopher who became a bishop of the Church of England. One of his unsuccessful projects was an attempt to found a college in the Bermudas for English colonists. The poem was in the air in the second half of the nineteenth century because of a line that served the purposes of the expansionist party in Congress: "Westward the course of empire takes its way." This was the Congress that passed the Morrill Act of 1862, which granted each state a piece of land for the establishment of a college devoted to agriculture and the mechanical arts. In 1864 the California legislature formally accepted 150,000 acres of the land the United States had wrested from the Republic of Mexico, and in 1867 they decided to locate the new university on the east shore of San Francisco Bay. A private school of higher education, the College of California had already been established in Oakland by a Massachusetts Congregationalist minister named Henry Durant, who had acquired 160 acres of land near Strawberry Creek. The two institutions merged, the classical college and the land-grant university became the University of California, and the town of Berkeley was given its name. The location of the university worried its first president, a Yale man named Daniel Coit Gilman. Berkeley, he said, had "no school, no practicing physician, and but few and indifferent stores. The walks and roads are in bad condition most of the year, and the inconveniences of family life are great." Nevertheless "time's noblest offspring" was launched.

GOING EAST

Elsewhere,
a babe's first words might be
ma ma, or da da
In Berkeley,
babies are born in a
lotus position
Their first word is
Karma
There might be more
Buddhists in Berkeley than
in Tibet
Some are from Tibet
but many are from
Brooklyn
Bishop George Berkeley
you got it backwards
It's "Go East, Young Man,
Go East."

    —Ishmael Reed

Ishmael Reed was born in Chattanooga, Tennessee, in 1938 and grew up in Buffalo, New York. He attended the University of Buffalo and worked for the city's black community newspaper, *Empire Star Weekly.* He moved to New York City in 1962 and helped establish *The East Village Other,* one of the country's first alternative tabloids. He arrived in Berkeley to teach at the university in 1967, the year of the publication of his first novel, *The Free-Lance Pallbearers,* and in a very short time he found his way to Oakland. Other novels followed: *Mumbo Jumbo, Yellow Back Radio Broke-Down, The Last Days of Louisiana Red, Reckless Eyeballing,* and his first book of poems, *Conjure,* which appeared in 1972. In the 1970s, together with Al Young, he founded and edited *Yardbird,* the country's first multicultural literary journal. He is the author—at last count—of nine novels, five books of poems, four plays, and five books of essays, including *Blues City: A Walk in Oakland.* In 1976 he founded the Before Columbus Foundation to promote a pan-cultural vision of American letters. He received a MacArthur fellowship in 1998. In this poem he remembers Bishop Berkeley and his popular interpreter, the New York journalist Horace Greeley, who advised U.S. citizens in the middle of the nineteenth century to head west.

Farewell San Miguel, splendid with your harvested fields
Where Angela de Trejo leaves her misty eyes.

Adiós San Miguel, lucido con sus milpas y rastrojos
Donde deja Angela de Trejo empañados sus ojos.

   —Angela de Trejo, upon leaving her native village for Alta California in 1776; translated by
   Antonio Mantilla Sanchez

Angela de Trejo was the mother-in-law of Luis Maria Peralta, who owned the land that became present-day Berkeley. Her couplet, saying goodbye to her village, survives in the Peralta family papers and is most of what is known about her. Peralta came to California with his parents in 1775 when he was sixteen and served as a soldier, and then an officer, in the garrisons at Monterey and San Francisco. In 1820 he was rewarded by the King of Spain with a grant of land that stretched from the bay to the crest of the hills and from San Leandro Creek in the south to Albany Hill in the north. At his death in 1842 he divided his rancho among his four grown sons. The northwest portion, which included Berkeley, Albany, and some of north Oakland, was given to José Domingo Peralta. After the United States annexed California, the new territory spawned thousands of lawsuits by the Yankee interlopers contesting the legality of the Mexican Californian land claims. Many, perhaps most, of the Californios lost their land by selling it off to pay their legal fees. Domingo Peralta sold all of Berkeley and Albany in 1853 for $82,000, except for three hundred acres he kept to himself near the present corner of Hopkins and Albina.

Sakai Harbor:
When ships from the foreign south
sailed to and fro
what a mingling of springs and
autumns there must have been

—Yosano Akiko, celebrating the diversity of the early days of Sakai, Berkeley's sister city; translated by Janine Beichman

The war between the United States and Japan for control of the Pacific began with the Japanese bombing of Pearl Harbor in 1941 and ended with the atomic bombs dropped by the United States on the cities of Hiroshima and Nagasaki. The bombs, which incinerated 200,000 people in a matter of moments, changed the world. They were designed and manufactured in laboratories under the supervision of the University of California. The Berkeley-Sakai Association, formed in 1967, was designed to promote cultural exchange and friendship between the two cities. Sakai is an ancient city, located on an inland sea in Osaka Prefecture. Until the seventeenth century it was a powerful merchant city and the nexus of international trading routes from Spain and Portugal that passed through the Philippines and Southeast Asia. Many Chinese, Korean, and other Asian immigrants lived there, making it one of the most culturally diverse of Japanese cities. This poem—sent to Berkeley by the city of Sakai for the Addison Street installation—celebrates the diversity of the early days of Sakai. It was written about the city of her birth by the poet **Yosano Akiko** (1878–1942).

THE DROUTH

From Shasta south to El Cajon,
    From Tahoe to the sea-girt shore,
No cloud in answer to our moan
    Bears prophecy of rain once more.

The north wind blows a bitter drouth,
    The west wind sweeps across the plain,
But O the wind of east and south
    Comes not with cheering sign of rain.

The herbage starts not on the hills,
    The cattle starve in pastures sear,
The fruit trees wilt and babbling rills
    Lapse off in sand and disappear.

O clouds of hope, O welcome wind,
    We pray thee kiss our fainting flowers;
To this fair fruitful land be kind
    And bless us with abundant showers.

—Charles Keeler

Charles Keeler (1871–1937) grew up in Milwaukee, Wisconsin. A passionate naturalist, he moved to Berkeley in his last year of high school and entered the university in 1893, having worked the summer before for the U.S. Biological Survey in the Sierra Nevada. He is an important and memorable figure in the early cultural history of the city. At the university he founded the Berkeley Evolution Club in 1890 and made friends with the painter William Keith and Joseph LeConte, the geology professor who was studying the formation of Yosemite Valley. He published his first scientific work, *Evolution of Colors of North American Land Birds*, in 1893; his interest in ornithology continued, and in 1899 he published a book of essays on the natural history of California entitled *Bird Notes Afield,* in which he gives the following description of the East Bay at the turn of the century:

> It is impossible to understand our birds without knowing something of their surroundings—of the lovely reach of ascending plain from the bay shore to the rolling slopes of the Berkeley Hills (mountains, our eastern friends call them); of the cold, clear streams of water which have cut their way from the hill crests into the plain, forming lovely cañons with great live-oaks in their lower and more open portions, and sweet-scented laurel or bay trees crowded into their narrower and more precipitous parts; of the great expanse of open hill slopes, green and tender during the months of winter rain, and soft brown and purple when the summer sun has parched the grass and flowers. These, with cultivated gardens and fields of grain, make the environment of our birds, and here they live their busy lives.

Although Keeler published many books of poems, printed by his own press called At the Sign of the Live Oak, he is best remembered for *Bird Notes Afield* and *The Simple House,* a book that promoted the ideas of William Morris, arguing for simplicity in domestic architecture, craftsmanship in design, and the use of local materials, which in Berkeley meant redwood shingle. The book became the bible of the Arts and Crafts Movement in California. It came out of his meeting with the young architect Bernard Maybeck, who built the newly married Keeler a house in 1895. Maybeck, Keeler, John Galen Howard (the chairman of the university's architecture department), and Howard's wife, Mary Robertson Bradbury, formed the Hillside Club to promote their ideas about the development of the city—which included the winding streets of the Berkeley hills, paths leading to cheap public transportation, simple homes made from natural materials, building sites that conformed to the landscape, and native plant gardening. Keeler and his wife also created a home-based arts and crafts guild where they produced their own furniture for sale in the Mission and Craftsman styles. Keeler served as managing director of the Berkeley Chamber of Commerce from 1920 to 1927 and in 1925 organized the First Berkeley Cosmic Society, whose purpose was to encourage research in the sciences and practice in the fine arts as the basis for a universal religion.

THE PURPLE COW

I never saw a purple cow,
I never hope to see one,
But I can tell you anyhow,
I'd rather see than be one.

—Gelett Burgess

Gelett Burgess (1866–1951) was born in Boston, attended MIT, became a draftsman for the Southern Pacific Railroad, and then in 1891 an instructor in topographical drawing at the eighteen-year-old University of California. From 1895 to 1897 he also edited a San Francisco literary magazine, *The Lark*, in which he published his best-known poem, "The Purple Cow," in 1895. He later moved to New York, where he lived for many years and where he published this poem:

THE PURPLE COW: SUITE

Ah, yes, I wrote the 'Purple Cow'—
I'm sorry now I wrote it;
But I can tell you anyhow,
I'll kill you if you quote it.

Burgess died in Carmel.

SUSIE ASADO

Sweet sweet sweet sweet sweet tea.
    Susie Asado.
Sweet sweet sweet sweet sweet tea.
    Susie Asado.
Susie Asado which is a told tray sure.
A lean on the shoe this means slips slips hers.
When the ancient light grey is clean it is yellow, it is a silver seller.
This is a please this is a please there are the saids to jelly. These are the
wets these say the sets to leave a crown to Incy.
Incy is short for incubus.
A pot. A pot is a beginning of a rare bit of trees. Trees tremble, the old
vats are in bobbles, bobbles which shade and shove and render clean, render clean must.
    Drink pups.
Drinks pups drink pups lease a sash hold, see it shine and a bobolink has pins.
It shows a nail.
What is a nail. A nail is unison.
Sweet sweet sweet sweet sweet tea.

    —Gertrude Stein

Gertrude Stein (1874–1946) was born in Allegheny, Pennsylvania, the youngest of five children. After living in France and Austria, her family settled in East Oakland in 1880, where her father, Daniel, took a seat on the San Francisco Stock Exchange and acquired an interest in San Francisco streetcar companies. Gertrude's mother died in 1888. She left high school without a diploma in 1889 and, after her father's death in 1891, moved to Baltimore, Maryland, to live with an aunt. She studied at Radcliffe and Johns Hopkins Medical School, leaving without a medical degree. She joined her brother Leo in Paris in 1903, met Henri Matisse and Pablo Picasso in 1905, and began to acquire their paintings. Her first book, *Three Lives,* was published in 1909. She went on to become the most famous experimental writer of her generation. "Susie Asado," one of her early experiments in cubist poetry, is said to be about a Spanish dancer she met and admired in Barcelona in 1910.

Stein described her childhood home in her 1925 work *The Making of Americans:*

It was an old place left over from when [Oakland] was just beginning. It was grounds about ten acres large, fenced in with just ordinary kind of rail fencing, it had a not very large wooden house standing on riding ground in the center with a winding avenue of eucalyptus, blue gum, leading from it to the gateway. There was, just around the house, a pleasant garden, in front were green lawns not very carefully attended and with large trees in the center whose roots always sucked up for themselves almost all the moisture, water in this dry western country could not be used just to keep things green and pretty and so, often, the grass was very dry in summer, but it was very pleasant then lying there watching the birds, black in the bright sunlight and sailing, and the firm white summer clouds breaking away from the horizon and slowly moving. It was very wonderful there in summer in the dry heat, and the sun burning, and the hot earth for sleeping; and then in the winter with the rain, and the north wind blowing that would bend the trees and often break them, and the owls in the walls scaring you with their tumbling. All the rest of the ten acres was for hay and a little vegetable gardening and an orchard with all the kinds of fruit trees that could be got there to do any growing.

DESERT CENTER

There's a magnet in the desert earth,
Or a meteor buried deep,
An old Indian said.
It fell there long ago,
A black star with a tail,
A long, lizard tail,
And it fell
To show
The earth people
Where the center was.
Deep down in the earth
It is there,
For it draws us
And it draws us,
And it draws you, too,
And you will always return.

    —Margaret Erwin Schevill

Margaret Erwin Schevill (1887–1962), poet, painter, and student of Navajo culture, was born in Jersey City, New Jersey, of mixed Irish and British ancestry. She grew up in a prosperous middle-class Episcopalian home and attended Wellesley College, from which she graduated in 1909. She took a job as an English teacher and girls' basketball coach at a high school in Tucson, Arizona, during which time she developed her abiding love of the Sonoran Desert and of Native American culture. On a vacation to California she met a Berkeley professor, Rudolph Schevill, and they were soon married and living in a redwood-shingled cottage on a canyon in the Berkeley hills. She had three children, the youngest of whom, James, also became a well-known Berkeley poet. Faculty wives interested in writing in those years used to meet during the day to share their writing (and babysitting). The group which included Schevill and Henriette Durham sometimes called themselves the Mother's Milk Club. Margaret Schevill's first book of poems, *Canyon Garden*, was published in 1921. In a rather stormy life that included an affair with Frank Lloyd Wright, psychoanalysis with Carl Jung in Zurich, and many years in the Southwest studying Hopi and Navajo art and mythology, she continued to write and paint. Her later publications include *Desert Sheaf* (1942) and a book that retells Navajo myths, *The Pollen Path* (1954).

AFTERMATH (1945)

All this is ended now. It is over and done,
The vigil, the waiting for news, the counting of days.
Now you may walk securely beneath the sun,
You may read, or sew, or dream in a still haze.

The nerves will slacken at length, their tension spent.
You will wonder what to do with limitless time
Now horror is ended, thankfully content
To juggle with words, to search for the apt rhyme.

But not for long. Not forever may one endure
The numbing of heart and sense by a sick shame.
You have lived these days. You will never be wholly sure
Of peace, or breath, or the sound of your own name.

—Henriette de S. Blanding

Henriette de Saussure Blanding was born in San Francisco in 1890. After graduating from Vassar, she returned to San Francisco to marry Chauncey Shafter Goodrich. They lived in the city until 1920, when they commissioned Julia Morgan to build them a home in Saratoga. They had four children. Henriette, who began to write poems as a young girl, was published in *Harper's Magazine* in the 1920s. After Chauncey's death in 1941, Henriette became wife to two Berkeley professors of English, first Willard Higley Durham, who died in 1955 and for whom Durham Theater on campus is named, and then Bejamin Lehman, who outlived her. At Berkeley she shared poems with Margaret Schevill and other members of what became known as the Mother's Milk Club and was the secret benefactor of the poet Muriel Rukeyser, who found herself pregnant and without work in Berkeley in the late 1940s. This poem, written in response to the end of the Second World War, comes from a volume of poems published by her children after her death.

IN TOPAZ

Can this hard earth break wide
   The stiff stillness of snow
And yield me promise that
   This is not always so?

Surely, the warmth of sun
   Can pierce the earth ice-bound,
Until grass comes to life,
   Outwitting barren ground!

   —Toyo Suyemoto

Toyo Suyemoto (1916–2003) was born in Oroville, California, one of eleven children of Tsutomu Howard Suyemoto and Mitsu Hyakusoku Suyemoto. She grew up in Sacramento and attended the University of California in the mid-1930s, majoring in English. In later years she spoke fondly of a course in Shakespeare she took with Professor Bertand Bronson. Her life changed when, after the Japanese bombing of Pearl Harbor in December 1941, the U.S. government issued the infamous Executive Order 9066, which required the relocation of all Japanese Americans living on the West Coast. Toyo Suyemoto was twenty-five years old when she reported with her son Kay and her family to Tanforan Racetrack, where they were housed in whitewashed horse stalls and eventually shipped to the Topaz Internment Camp in Utah. In Topaz, while one of her brothers fought in the U.S. Army, she became the camp librarian, taught school, and participated in a writing group. Her son Kay, aged sixteen, died from severe allergies linked to horse dander and other irritants, to which he was exposed during the family's internment. Released in 1945, the family moved to Cincinnati, where Toyo worked as reference librarian at the Cincinnati Museum and at the nursing school of the University of Cincinnati. She received an MA in library science from the University of Michigan and became the head of the Social Work Library at Ohio State University in Columbus. She was associated with the National Council for Japanese American Redress and testified before a congressional committee about her experience in Topaz, which is also chronicled in the documentary *Days of Remembrance*. Her poems and reminiscences appear in *Quiet Fire: A Historical Anthology of Asian American Poetry, 1892–1970* and *Last Witnesses: Reflections on the Wartime Internment of Japanese Americans*.

POEM ABOUT MYSELF

Usury drove my parents from the house
    Where I was born
(Abandoned, it grew rotten, windows broke;
Finally, on a calm day, it collapsed
    From its usurious load).
The place they found was in a useless desert
Where plants were homilies on being poor,
    And beasts on being low.
This happened two changed lives ago, when I
    Thought childhood best ignored.

Engineers came and drove us from our desert,
    Expensive, offhand men;
They tore up trees, dug valleys, moved a hill
With their new truck- and tripod-faith, and built
    Dams in the arid land.
Two hundred miles and through a range of mountains
They brought a river, and poured a lake upon
    Our moral, desert home.
Under the engineers' lake the countryside
    Of my changed youth has gone.

    —George P. Elliott

George P. Elliott (1918–1980) was born in Knightstown, Indiana. His family moved from the Midwest to southern California in the 1920s, where his father bought a farm and grew carobs, a tropical plant touted as a healthy alternative to chocolate. It was the archetypal pattern of migration in those years, and attempting a tropical plantation in an arid climate was an archetypal California enterprise, which Elliott would write about in an essay entitled "Coming of Age on the Carob Plantation." He entered UC Berkeley in 1935, studied with Josephine Miles, and received a BA in 1939 and an MA in 1941. He was employed as a steelworker and a labor reporter during the war years and belonged to a group of East Bay writers and artists that included James Schevill and the photographer Dorothea Lange. He taught at St. Mary's College in Moraga from 1947 to 1955, went east to teach at Barnard College in New York from 1957 to 1960 and at the Iowa Writers' Workshop in 1960 and 61, and returned to teach at UC Berkeley and St. Mary's for a year in 1962 and 1963, after which he directed the writing program of Syracuse University. He is best known for his novels and short stories about Berkeley and the East Bay. They include a trilogy of novels, *Parktilden Village, David Knudsen,* and *In the World,* and two volumes of stories, *Among the Dangs* and *An Hour of Last Things.* A book of poems, *From the Berkeley Hills,* was published in 1969.

In all of his East Bay books, Elliott is fascinated with architecture. In his 1963 novel *In the World,* he describes the changing aesthetic of the homes in the Berkeley hills:

San Jacinto Way was a short, winding street half a mile north of the campus in Berkeley. The street curled on a deep ledge part way up the range of steep hills against which the city backed to the east; some of the houses on the uphill side of the ledge, among them the Royces', had a glimpse of the Bay and the Golden Gate. The long-time residents of the street were well-agreed that a panoramic view of the Bay was vastly overrated and that, if they were forced to live in the celebrated, extremely modern, cliff-hanging houses further up on the hill, they would not enjoy the panorama assaulting them from the west but would be forced to protect themselves from it. They thought it ostentatious to pull back the curtain and expose the grand view to a guest's involuntary admiration. They preferred to let him find for himself the bonsai maple in the dented copper tub, the bird-of-paradise plant below the terrace, the fact that a disarrayed hillside garden was composed entirely of California natives.

LOVE SONG IN SUMMER'S FURNACE HEAT

Let the white blossoms blow,
my love is gone
and summer's furnace heat rolls on.

Let the white blossoms blow.
Hell lines the freeways
with fumes of foul days.

Let the white blossoms blow
telling when my love returns,
love learns when it burns.

—James Schevill

James Schevill was born in Berkeley in 1920, where his father, Rudolph Schevill, had founded the university's romance languages department. James graduated from Harvard in 1942 and then served four years in the Army, the last two with the secret "Reeducation of German Prisoners of War" program. (There were 350,000 German prisoners of war in the United States). Schevill had had a previous encounter with Nazism in 1938 when he visited a college friend who was an exchange student at the University of Freiburg and witnessed the arrest of a rabbi and the burning of a synagogue on what turned out to be Kristallnacht. After his discharge from the Army, a job awaited him teaching at University of California Extension, but he refused to sign the recently imposed loyalty oath required of all university instructors and went to work instead at the California College of Arts and Crafts and then at San Francisco State, where from 1961 to 1968 he served as director of the Poetry Center. In 1968 he became a professor of English at Brown University, and upon his retirement in 1985 he and his wife, Margot, moved back to Berkeley. Poet and playwright, his major publications include two volumes of collected poems from 1962 and 1968, a *New and Selected Poems* from 2000, and several editions of his plays.

HEIGHT

The heron moonlight feathers the full air.

Across the light lying like unturned feathers
I see the precipice night.
The waters clear. What was not clear before
Is clear with a clearness of cliffs.

Flying is strict and casual.
The snow storm in its glass breaks harder
Than moons their swan snow.

   Considering
How all the slow birds go from us
In their own slipped-axe minute of flying.

   —Rosalie Moore

Rosalie Moore (1910–2001) was born in Oakland to a railroad man and a teacher. She attended the University of California from 1928 to 1934, earning a BA and an MA in English. In the depths of the Depression she found a job working as an announcer and copywriter at the Oakland radio station KLX, writing verse drama in her spare time. One of her plays won the University of Chicago's Sergel Drama Prize in 1938. In the 1940s and 50s, she was associated with the Activists, a group of Berkeley poets and one of the first to organize themselves as a self-conscious literary movement, whose leader, Lawrence Hart, taught a poetry class from his Berkeley home. Hart preached that poems should be exciting, with every line active. Other members of the group included Robert Horan, Jeanne McGahey, and Bill Brown, whom Moore married in 1942. Her first book of poems, *The Grasshopper's Man and Other Poems*, was selected by W. H. Auden for the Yale Younger Poets series in 1948. Beginning in the early 1950s Brown and Moore, who had moved to Marin County, collaborated on a series of children's books. She taught at the College of Marin from 1965 to 1976. Her other books of poems include *Year of the Children, Of Singles and Doubles,* and *Gutenberg in Strasbourg*. She died in Petaluma.

WE ARE LIKE THESE THINGS

We walk alone on the beach.
Two ships sail by.
The gulls are thick as snow on the rocks;
And the light is sorrowful in the sky.

The purpose of life is hidden and grey as the clouds
That sniff at the high rocks like white hounds.
Life is fragmentary and brief as the clouds
And the toppling sand mounds.

Surely we are like these things that touch us:
The half tones, this cool pleasant wind,
The shells drying on the sands, the straggling sea-weed.
We are like these things, impermanent and unpinned.

    —Madeline Gleason

Madeline Gleason (1903–1979) was a poet, playwright, and painter. She was born in Fargo, North Dakota, and toured as a child, singing and tap dancing in the vaudeville circuits of the Midwest. She moved to Portland and in 1935 to San Francisco, making her living for a while in San Francisco's financial district as a runner in the Stock Exchange. Her first book, *Poems*, appeared in 1944 and in those years she became a part of the poetry group in Berkeley that included Robert Duncan and Jack Spicer. In 1947 she organized an event she called the First Festival on Modern Poetry, which featured a public reading by Kenneth Rexroth, Duncan, and Spicer. Duncan's play, *Mrs. Noah*, is said to be about her. Her second book, *The Metaphysical Needle*, from which this poem is taken, appeared in 1949.

HOMAGE TO A TOM-CAT

Rainy, sore at the whole town,
Its committees and longings,
I look on plum-tree branches,
New white blossoms, dripping water,
Tap on my study window.
My official paper days
Are done by another man.
I exist only here. Night
Finds me a little drunk. Wife,
Child, and I, affectionate
And calm with each other's love
Eat well as the town lights up
Electric, frenetic, bright.
Our cat has been gone three weeks.
He came to us from nowhere
And has gone back to nowhere,
And I return to poems
that observe the same process
Yet love never seems pointless.

—Thomas Parkinson

Thomas Parkinson (1920–1992) was born in San Francisco. He attended UC Berkeley, where he studied poetry with Josephine Miles and received a BA in 1945 and a PhD in 1948. He taught in the English department there from 1948 until his retirement in 1991. As a graduate student he was a member of Kenneth Rexroth's Anarchist Circle and, through his friendship with the Berkeley poets Robert Duncan, Jack Spicer, and Robin Blaser, he came to know, and to provide academic sponsorship to, many of the Beat generation writers. He was a scholar of the Irish poet William Butler Yeats and published two books about him, *W. B. Yeats: Self-Critic* and *W. B. Yeats: The Later Poetry*, both published by the University of California Press. He also published *A Casebook on the Beat* in 1961, a volume that gave some academic respectability to the new writers. His own poems were gathered in *Collected Poems,* published by Oyez Press in 1980, and *Poems: New and Selected,* published by the National Poetry Foundation. A tall man, he was an electric presence on the campus, and he and his wife, Ariel, were very much political activists, for which Parkinson paid a price: In 1961, a mentally ill former student who decided to do something about the Communist menace walked into Parkinson's office with a sawed-off shotgun and fired it point-blank. The student with Parkinson was killed and half of Parkinson's face was blown off, but he survived and resumed teaching. He taught poetry to four generations of Berkeley students and continued to support controversial causes.

WIND, CLOUDS, AND THE DELICATE CURVE OF THE WORLD

Wind, clouds, and the delicate curve of the world
Stretching so far away . . .
On a cloud in the clear sight of heaven
Sit Kali and Jesus, disputing.
Tree shadows, cloud shadows
Falling across the body of the world
That sleeps with one arm thrown across her eyes . . .
A wind stirs in the daisies
And trees are sighing,
"These houses and these gardens are illusions."
Leaf shadows, cloud shadows,
And the wind moving as far as the eye can reach . . .

—Louis Simpson

Louis Simpson was born in Jamaica, West Indies, in 1923. He immigrated to the United States and studied at Columbia College. During World War II he served with the 101st Airborne Division in Europe. In 1949 he published his first book of poems, *The Arrivistes*. He worked as an editor in New York, a teacher at Columbia, and then, beginning in 1959, at UC Berkeley. In 1964 a book of his Berkeley poems, *At the End of the Open Road*, was awarded the Pulitzer Prize for poetry. He left Berkeley in 1967 for the State University of New York at Stony Brook. He has published over the years seventeen volumes of poetry, criticism, translation, and memoir. One of his memorable images of Berkeley is a description of the plum trees in the hills in February:

And the angel at the gate, the flowering plum,
Dances like Italy,
Imagining red.

THE ELECTION

How did the stones vote
this time?

They voted for hardness
and few words

as the trees voted
for slow growth
upward and a shedding
of dead dependents.

And the men?

They voted against
themselves again
and for fire
which they thought they
could control,
fire
which voted for blackened stumps
and no more elections.

—Leonard Nathan

Leonard Nathan, born in Los Angeles in 1924, came to Berkeley in 1948 after a stint in the U.S. Army. He received his BA, MA, and PhD in English at Berkeley, taught several years at Modesto Junior College, and returned to Berkeley to teach in the Department of Speech, of which, when it was transformed into the Department of Rhetoric, he served as chair. He retired in 1992. He has published eleven books of poetry and a study of W. B. Yeats; translated a classic of Sanskrit poetry, the Meghaduta of Kalidasa, under the title *The Transport of Love;* collaborated with his friend Arthur Quinn on a study of Czeslaw Milosz's poetry; collaborated with Milosz on a translation of the Polish poet Anna Swir; and written, after he retired, *Diary of a Left-Handed Birdwatcher,* the second book of field ornithology produced by a Berkeley poet. (The first was Charles Keeler's *Bird Notes Afield* in 1899).

DANGEROUS GAMES

I fly a black kite on a long string.
As I reel it in,
I see it is a tame bat.
You say it's you.

You fly a white kite, but the string snaps.
As it flutters down,
You see it is a cabbage butterfly.
I say it's I.

You invented this game,
Its terms, its terminology.
I supplied the string,
Giving you the frayed length
So I could escape.

I flew a black kite, let go the string,
But the thing darted down
Straight for my long hair
To be entangled there.

You flew a white kite that ran away.
You chased it with your bat sonar.
But you found only a cabbage butterfly
Trembling on an aphid-riddled leaf.

   —Carolyn Kizer

Carolyn Kizer was born in Spokane, Washington, in 1925. She graduated from Sarah Lawrence College, lived in China, where her father was in the diplomatic service in mid-1940s, and did graduate work in poetry with Theodore Roethke at the University of Washington. In 1959 she founded, with David Wagoner, the magazine *Poetry Northwest*. She served as a cultural attaché to the U.S. Embassy in Pakistan in 1964 and 65 and served as the first director of the literature program of the National Endowment for the Arts from 1966 to 1970. In 1975 she married the architect and city planner John Woodbridge and moved to Berkeley. Her books include *The Ungrateful Garden, Knock Upon Silence,* and *Yin: New Poems,* for which she won the Pulitzer Prize in 1985. In recent years she and her husband have divided their time between their home in Sonoma and an apartment just off the Left Bank in Paris.

HOME FREE

Inch by inch along the bed,
Growing more compact, his arms pulled up like bird's wings
(My father is almost ninety),
I love you, I say, over and over,
Until I read in *Time Magazine* that saying this holds the dying back.
They get polite; they hang around to thank you.
I love you, I say,
Under my breath.

In Bangkok you can buy a bird in front of the temple
For twenty cents. It's not to eat
Nor to listen to nor to admire but to
Set free.
Spring the door with your plastic Diner's Card, wait for the scrabble, the
Head poked out the door, air by your face,
And up he goes.

    —Diana O'Hehir

Diana O'Hehir was born in Lexington, Virginia, in 1922 and was brought to Berkeley at the age of one by her parents. She attended UC Berkeley for a year and a half and studied poetry with Josephine Miles. After dropping out of school, she worked from 1946 to 1948 as a union organizer for the Congress of Industrial Organizations (CIO), and applied to Johns Hopkins University in the early 1950s for a program that allowed her to begin graduate study without a BA. She took her MA from Hopkins, and in 1958 completed a PhD. She taught English and creative writing at Mills College for thirty-two years and also headed those programs. She and Chana Bloch, her colleague at Mills, shared poems back and forth almost daily over many years. She is the author of two novels, *I Wish This War Were Over* and *The Bride Who Ran Away*, and several books of poems, including *Summoned, The Power to Change Geography, Home Free,* and most recently *Spells for Not Dying Again,* which received the 1997 Bay Area Book Reviewers Award. After living for many years in Kensington and Berkeley, she now lives in San Francisco with her husband, Mel Fiske.

NATURAL HISTORY

It takes a long time to make a meadow.
First you need glaciers
to gouge out a lake.
Then reeds grow, the lake fills with silt and mud
and finally grass.

It takes a long time to have a feeling,
even the ones that come quickly.

So many trees with their litter
of fallen leaves to beget
a single joy that turns to the light.
Look at the broken hopes up and down that trunk.
Each one could have been a branch.

What a terrible gulf between heart
and mouth.
         And the words fall
like belated raindrops
the day after a storm when you shake the tree,
if you happen to shake it.

    —Chana Bloch

Chana Bloch was born in New York City in 1940. She came to Berkeley in 1967 and has taught for many years at Mills College, where she also served as director of the creative writing program. She has written three books of poems, *The Secrets of the Tribe, The Past Keeps Changing,* and *Mrs. Dumpty.* She is co-translator of the ancient Hebrew *The Song of Songs* as well as several volumes by contemporary Israeli poets: Dahlia Ravikovitch's *A Dress of Fire* and *The Window,* and Yehuda Amichai's *Selected Poetry* and *Open Closed Open.*

THE UNSWEPT

Broken bay leaf. Olive pit.
Crab leg. Claw. Crayfish armor.
Whelk shell. Mussel shell. Dogwinkle. Snail.
Wishbone tossed unwished on. Test
of sea urchin. Chicken foot.
Wrasse skeleton. Hen head
—eye shut, beak open
as if singing in the dark. Laid down in tiny
tiles, by the rhyparographer,
each scrap has a shadow,—each shadow cast
by a different light. Permanently fresh
husks of the feast! When the guest has gone,
the morsels dropped on the floor are left
as food for the dead—O my characters,
my imagined, here are some fancies of crumbs
from under love's table.

    —Sharon Olds

Sharon Olds was born in San Francisco in 1942 and grew up in Berkeley. She attended Berkeley High and Stanford University, graduating in 1964. She moved to New York, went to graduate school in English at Columbia University, married, and had two children. She is the author of a number of books of poetry, including *Satan Says; The Dead and the Living* (which received the National Book Critics Circle Award in poetry in 1984); *The Gold Cell; The Father; The Wellspring; Blood, Tin, Straw;* and most recently *The Unswept Room.* For many years she has taught in the creative writing program at New York University and has returned to California in the summers to teach in the Squaw Valley Community of Writers Poetry Workshop.

THE EYE BEHIND THE I

From here, I can go anywhere
Anchored to this desk, I see
three narcissus in a slender pewter vase

On the floor by my feet is my black bag
with its white clown faces,
empty now of my teaching tricks, it sags

French doors open out to campus
past trees, buildings, the town
out, out across the land

then up, up past clouds, up
out to the universe
planets, stars, galaxies, black holes

then I return, see again the desk
a highly glazed fat cup holds
pens that free my imagination

to soar   to soar

—Adam David Miller

Adam David Miller was born in 1922 in South Carolina. He came to Berkeley in 1944 as a member of a World War II U.S. Navy unit stationed at International House. He returned to the university after the war, received two degrees in English, and did post-master's work in dramatic literature. *Occident,* the campus literary magazine, published his first poem. While at UC Berkeley, he also helped found *The Graduate Student Journal* and served as its first editor. He has published five books of verse, including *Forever Afternoon,* which won the first Naomi Long Madgett Award for poetry. He has served for many years on the Berkeley Civic Arts Commission and had a hand in the creation of the Addison Street Anthology.

IN THESE DARK TIMES

You must feel loved when you read this.
Lean against the hand
stroking the back of your neck. Relax.
In the pocket where you once kept marbles
is a small bag full of kisses.
Open it. Let it go.
Someone's humming in the next room
with a throaty laugh at every missed note
because mistakes don't matter.
No, don't go see.
You don't even have to listen.
You are loved.
There's a warm smell coming from the kitchen
and the puppy's nibbling your slippers
but you're too comfortable to get angry.
There are so many people who want this.
Just this.
Believe me, they are not your enemies.

—Julia Vinograd

Julia Vinograd was born in Berkeley in 1943 and grew up in Pasadena. She attended UC Berkeley from 1961 to 1965 and then received an MFA at the University of Iowa Writers' Workshop. She came back to Berkeley just in time for the People's Park uprising and quickly became one of the most familiar faces in the vivid street life of Telegraph Avenue. Every year for thirty years she has written a book of what she calls "street poems." She publishes the books herself and has sold them on "the Avenue," where, in a bright yellow slouch cap, long braid, and gypsy assemblage of clothing, she blows bubbles from the little wire dumbbell of a child's bubble-blowing kit and hawks her wares. Her dress and the liveliness of her poems has remained unchanged, and she has come to seem both emblem and survivor of the flower-child Berkeley of the 1960s. The students at the university call her "The Bubble Lady"; she has often been called, also, the poet laureate of the city.

BASEBALL AND CLASSICISM

Every day I peruse the box scores for hours
Sometimes I wonder why I do it
Since I am not going to take a test on it
And no one is going to give me money

The pleasure's something like that of codes
Of deciphering an ancient alphabet say
So as brightly to picturize Eurydice
In the Elysian Fields on her perfect day

The day she went 5 for 5 against Vic Raschi

 —Tom Clark

Tom Clark was born in Oak Park, Illinois, in 1941. In his teenage years he worked as a baseball usher in Chicago. He graduated from the University of Michigan, did postgraduate work at Cambridge and Essex in England, then in 1967 returned to the United States. He lived first in New York, where he was associated with the New York School of poets, and then in Bolinas, which was turning into a haven for poets and artists in the late 1960s. From 1963 to 1973 he was poetry editor of *The Paris Review*. He moved to Berkeley with his family in 1984 and since then has been a core faculty member of the program in poetics at New College in San Francisco. *Sleepwalker's Fate: New and Selected Poems, 1965–1991* was published in 1992. A painter as well as a poet, Clark is also a gifted literary biographer, having written lives of Damon Runyon, Jack Kerouac, Ted Berrigan, Louis Ferdinand Céline, Charles Olson, Robert Creeley, and Edward Dorn.

Vic Raschi was a right-handed pitcher for the New York Yankees from 1946 to 1953. A four-time All Star, he was undefeated in World Series competition, winning six games. In Greek mythology, Eurydice was the wife of the poet Orpheus, who tried and failed to bring her back from the land of the dead.

A CHILDHOOD AROUND 1950

Sometimes a horse pulled a wagon down the street.
A knife-grinder sometimes knocked at the back door.
Airplanes passed over. Put to bed in the poignant
half-thereness of summer twilights, we followed their long wobble
into Midway, rare and slow as dragonflies.

New kinds of safety. Our parents held their breath,
though sickness, for us, was the vile yellow powders
that burst from the capsules we had to gulp, and couldn't.
The new danger quiet in the milk and air.

The electric chair troubled no one. Good and evil
were stark things, as grainy movies made the dark.
But the city stopped if one of us was stolen,
and found thrown, days later, in a forest preserve.

It was what was. A childhood always is.
Fathers came home at noon and took off their hats.
Later, streetlights . . . But who was that *lamplighter*, in the stories?
And we went on living it, like a wave, that doesn't know
it is at every moment different water.

    —Alan Williamson

Alan Williamson was born in Chicago in 1944, grew up there, and spent his summers on the Monterey peninsula, where his maternal grandparents lived. He went east to school, to Haverford and then Harvard, where he studied poetry with Robert Lowell. In the 1970s and early 1980s he taught at the University of Virginia, Harvard, and Brandeis, and then, after two years in Europe, came west in 1982 to teach at UC Davis, settling a year later in Berkeley. His literary friends, with whom he met regularly in the 80s and 90s to critique poems, included Peter Dale Scott, Sandra Gilbert, and Jeanne Foster. Brought up Episcopalian, he became a practicing Zen Buddhist in the late 80s. His books include four volumes of poetry—*Presence, The Muse of Distance, Love and the Soul,* and *Res Publica*—and four books of literary criticism.

THE CELL *from* SELF-PORTRAITS AT THE HEALTH MUSEUM

Every misconception, foolish
wish, and memory of the sea
begins here, inside a membrane-
bound sac of cytoplasm, where
endoplasmic reticulum forms
channels studded with beads.
The nucleus, round and yellow
as a grapefruit on the display,
is filled with helical DNA
encoding all the faults I got
from my parents—insomnia,
fear of water and elevators,
obsession with details, vanity.
Mitochondria spew out ATP
as proteins grow and fold,
following orders from RNA.
This is the machinery of
the soul, where love arises
as a series of electrical signals
mediated by ions traversing
the membrane, and sometimes
small epiphanies break free.

—Lucille Lang Day

Lucille Lang Day was born in Oakland in 1947. She attended UC Berkeley from 1967 to 1979, receiving a BA in biological sciences, an MA in zoology, and a PhD in science and math education. She also, during these years, studied poetry with Josephine Miles and joined the Berkeley Poets' Co-op. She later also earned an MA in creative writing at San Francisco State. Her poetry collections include *Infinities, Wild One, Fire in the Garden,* and *Self-Portrait with a Hand Microscope,* which received the Henry Joseph Jackson Award. She is director of the Hall of Health, a Berkeley museum, and the founder and director of Scarlet Tanager Books.

FIRST LIGHT

Graying chest hair emerging from his apron-top in tufts
dusted with a snow of flour
above the swelling rondure of his oven belly,
sleeves rolled, arms folded, at ease on the porch steps
outside the back door of the bakery

in the lively air of the early hour taking a break
while the bread cools on racks inside
and a breeze picks up off the bay: the mist lifts
and the swarming dust of starlight reappears,
the constellations that were given names

beside the hive-domed ovens of Chaldea and of Ur—
near first light, thick arms cradling rolls
and crusty loaves, a gift for late-returning revelers,
for the derelict who washes in the creek
under the bridge his daily bread at daybreak.

    —Jim Powell

Jim Powell was born in Berkeley in 1951 and grew up in the Santa Clara Valley, where both sides of his family had settled in the early years of the twentieth century. He returned to Berkeley in 1975, where he has lived ever since. A poet and translator of poetry from ancient Greek, Latin, French, and other languages, his publications include *It Was Fever That Made the World* and *Sappho: A Garland*. Among his honors is a MacArthur fellowship.

IN THE NEW WORLD

My mother in her Old World pose
sails through a shop on Third Avenue
like a steam liner, leaving froths
of lace, long white scarves in her wake.

She dons fur caps, high boarskin boots,
brocaded gowns of her Moscow youth;
like crystal, turning, decades flash
in velvet-curtained booths.

Once from her closet rack, I stole
a sequined shawl, black sash.
She laughed—to find me rouged
and stumbling in her spike-heeled shoes.

Now each, in turn, holds up a chipped
hand mirror for the other's use.
She tucks in strands of grey.
We pick out matching pins.

   —Florence Elon

A native New Yorker, **Florence Elon** took undergraduate courses at both the City College of New York and UC Berkeley, where she studied with Josephine Miles and Thom Gunn. She was a Stegner Fellow in poetry at Stanford, where she studied with Donald Davie, and a Fulbright Fellow in music at the University of London. She completed her PhD at Berkeley in 1976 and was a visiting writer at Yale and Northwestern before returning to the Bay Area in 1980, where she has taught creative writing at San Francisco State and UC Berkeley. A book of her poems, *Self-Made*, was published in 1984.

THE SKELETON'S DEFENSE OF CARNALITY

Truly I have lost weight, I *have*
lost weight,
grown lean in love's defense,
in love's defense grown grave.
It was concupiscence
that brought me to the state:
all bone and a bit of skin
to keep the bone within.

Flesh is no heavy burden
for one possessed of little
and accustomed to its loss.
I lean to love, which leaves me lean
till lean turn into lack.

A wanton bone, I sing my song
and travel where the bone is blown
and extricate true love from lust
as any man of wisdom must.

Then wherefore should I rage
against this pilgrimage
from gravel unto gravel?
Circuitous I travel
from love to lack
and lack to lack,
from lean to lack
and back.

  —Jack Foley

Jack Foley was born in Neptune, New Jersey, in 1940 and grew up in Port Chester, New York. After undergraduate studies at Cornell, he made his way across the country in 1963 with his wife, Adelle, to attend graduate school in English at Berkeley. "The Skeleton's Defense of Carnality" was written during those years, while Foley was working as manager of Edward Landberg's Cinema/Guild, Telegraph Avenue's legendary repertory movie house for which the future film critic Pauline Kael wrote the program notes. Foley had, meanwhile, plunged into Berkeley literary culture, coordinating poetry readings at Larry Blake's restaurant, then at Café Milano—both Berkeley fixtures, to which he often brought his friend, the poet Larry Eigner. In 1988 Foley began to produce programs—primarily about poetry—on Berkeley's listener-supported radio station KPFA. His readings came to feature choral pieces performed with his wife. Among his books are *Letters/Lights—Words for Adelle, Gershwin, Saint James* (a collaboration with Ivan Arguelles), and two critical works, *O Powerful Western Star* and *Foley's Books*. Most of his books have been published by Pantograph Press, a Berkeley publisher.

THE WORLD

My ears (shaped just like his)
echo too loudly, everything too
much, turtle, without my shell.
I am a gong that has been
unstruck. Still reverberating
from what is taken away, and
never was. A thousand sharp
leaves press against the window,
that tide, the clank of my spoon
against the blue china mug,

it doesn't take much
to make music.

    —Alice Jones

Alice Jones moved to Berkeley from New York in 1978 for a one-year job—a medical internship at Highland Hospital—and stayed. Her books include *The Knot, Isthmus, Extreme Directions,* and *Gorgeous Mourning.* She has received awards for her poetry from the National Endowment for the Arts and the Poetry Society of America. She practices psychoanalysis in Oakland and is co-editor, with Edward Smallfield, of Apogee Press.

BECAUSE WE NEED GOOD MAPS

   At this age of his when he wasn't here,

I study my imagination for the father
of the nine-year-old me, the adventures

   exciting him way off across a globe

with no country on it named Viet Nam.
I have to go find him, the man who came back

   a stranger. My father must still be roaming,

charting lost locations for this year of mine
which marks the journey I can't start.

   —Forrest Hamer

Forrest Hamer was born in Goldsboro, North Carolina, in 1956 and grew up there during the first stirrings of the civil rights movement. He came to Berkeley in 1978 to attend graduate school in psychology and has lived in the Bay Area ever since, conducting a psychotherapy practice and teaching occasionally in UC Berkeley's psychology department. His books of poems include *Call and Response* and *Middle Ear*. About this poem he remarks: "When I was a child I had an outdated globe in my bedroom that did not show 'Vietnam'; instead, it listed the old 'Indochina.' When my father went away to war, this added to my confusion about where it was he was going to be."

CAFFE MEDITERRANEUM

To get to the Med on the dream map of Berkeley
I had to abandon my body of a child and learn
to operate my body of an old man. I had to crawl
through poison oak and coyote-brush dripping with ticks,
on hillside game-paths where I saw the city burning.
In my dream, the café was still there at the center
of the earth, in media terrarium, and the same bearded
regulars from forty years ago were still chewing the fat
over the same cappucino in the same corner (biographies
in genetic wreckage of those marble tables, chipped,
kissed, burned and lost and never to be deciphered).
When I hit town, if you were truly hip you still called it
the Piccolo, and when I ran in breathless one afternoon
in Feb. 1969 to break the ageless hush and yell "they're
using tear gas on campus!" not one head turned to listen,
but I would have to accept birth and let go of death before I
could begin to understand this dispassionate wisdom.
Passionate wisdom? the denizens of the street are fresh out,
and I'm not sure I accept any definition of community
large enough to include me, but you never know where
the heart is until they amputate. Once the Med disappears
I don't know what fires I will have to crawl through
or what lives I may negotiate to get back there.

—John Oliver Simon

John Oliver Simon is a fifth-generation Californian who was born in New York City in 1942 and has lived in Berkeley since 1964. His great-great grandfather, Henry Perrin Coon, was Mayor of San Francisco in the 1860s and his great-grandfather, Emil Kehrlein, owned the largest whorehouse on the Barbary Coast before the 1906 earthquake. After completing a BA at Swarthmore College in Pennsylvania, Simon moved to Berkeley for graduate studies in English. He is a veteran of the free speech movement and of the People's Park uprising. He has translated many Latin American poets and has taught several generations of East Bay youngsters through California Poets in the Schools and Poetry Inside Out.

WHO I AM IN TWILIGHT

Like John Lee Hooker, like Lightnin Hopkins,
like the blues himself, the trickster sonnet,
hoedown, the tango, the *cante jondo,*
like blessed spirituals and ragas custom-made,
like novels, like stories, like slick, slow
sly soliloquies sliding into novels,
like Crime & Punishment, like death & birth,
Canal Street, New Orleans, like eased,
erasable, troubled voices a whirling
ceiling fan makes in deep summer nights in
hot unheavenly hotels, Oklahoma, Arkansas,
Tennessee, like the Mississippi River
so deep and wide you couldn't get a letter
to the other side, like Grand Canyon,
like Yosemite National Park, like beans &
cornbread, like rest & recreation, like love
& like, I know we last. I know our bleeding stops.

—Al Young

Al Young, novelist, essayist, and poet, was born in Ocean Springs, Mississippi, in 1939 and grew up in Detroit. He attended the University of Michigan from 1957 to 1961 and came to California in 1961. He took a Stegner fellowship in writing at Stanford in 1966 and then went to UC Berkeley to complete a second BA, this time in Spanish, in 1969. During this time he was an instructor in the Berkeley Youth Corps program and founded, with Ishmael Reed, the literary magazine *Yardbird,* which they published from 1972 to 1976. Young was an instructor at Stanford from 1969 to 1976 and has since been a visiting teacher at UC Berkeley and St. Mary's College. His first book of poems, *Dancing,* appeared in 1969, and his first novel, *Snakes,* in 1970. His other novels include *Sitting Pretty, Who Is Angelina?,* and *Seduction by Light.* His collected poems, *Heaven: Collected Poems 1958–1988,* appeared in 1989. He has also written a series of nonfiction books about his relationship to music that he describes as musical memoirs. They include *Bodies and Soul* and *Kinds of Blue.* He lives in Berkeley.

HOLY BODY

Late night fog
glows in the bay
like a holy body.
Morning slant
restores the trees
chalk white city
glass blue water.
By evening flushed
and spent
you grow dark again.
Mysterious and
constant lover.

—Susan Griffin

Susan Griffin was born in Los Angeles in 1943. As a girl she came to Berkeley to visit her older sister, and, she has written, the memory of its cafés and bookstores helped her survive high school. She returned to study at the university in 1960 and joined Slate, the anti-McCarthy, pro–civil rights student organization that became the seedbed of the free speech movement. Years later she would co-write the script for the documentary *Berkeley in the Sixties*. After attending UC Berkeley, she studied creative writing at San Francisco State with Robert Creeley and Kay Boyle and worked as an editorial assistant for *Ramparts* magazine. She moved back to Berkeley in 1966. Her first books of poems were published by local feminist presses that had sprung up in Berkeley in the 1970s—Alta's Shameless Hussy Press, Ma Ma Press, and Effie's. Her first play, *Voices,* had a public reading at Bacchanalia, the Oakland lesbian bar where Ntozake Shange's *For Colored Girls…* also premiered. Her later books of poems include *Like the Iris of an Eye, Unremembered Country,* and *Bending Home*. She has also been an influential writer of philosophical prose, including *Woman and Nature* and *A Chorus of Stones: The Private Life of War*. In 2003, with her Berkeley writer friends Alice Walker and Maxine Hong Kingston, Griffith was arrested in front of the White House in an act of civil disobedience protesting the war in Iraq.

AMAZING GRACE

A few words
                from the hymn
as I first heard it, in 1964,
arrested, after so much
church Latin, by the vulgate
pouring from the marchers' mouths.

October sun. Almost children,
in a game, sitting
around a police car.
The scene
                drenched in song

        someone who unfolds
        a letter, not to read it,
        but to see the shape
        of the handwriting again

the whole machine stalled in that moment.

—Edward Smallfield

232

Edward Smallfield was born in Sacramento in 1946 and attended UC Berkeley from 1964 to 1968 in the midst of the free speech movement and the developing counterculture of those years. After graduate study at the State University of New York at Buffalo, he settled permanently in Berkeley in 1974 and worked as a manager and public relations specialist for the San Francisco office of the Social Security Administration. His books include *The Pleasures of C, Trio* (with Tony Mirosevich and Charlotte Muse), and *One Hundred Famous Views of Edo* (with Doug MacPherson). With Alice Jones he is the co-editor of Apogee Press.

O BLANCA VIRGEN

Oh, pure virgin, come to your window.
Come to the balcony, listen to me.
      Sir, I shall scarcely hear your singing;
      Men's songs have no hold on my heart;
      My heart is a nest of its own enchantment;
      It lives in the heights, alone, apart.
Then by magic I'll turn into an eagle;
Into that heaven on wings I'll lunge!
      No sir—into a golden fish I'll change me,
      And swiftly into the ocean plunge.
Virgin, I'll turn into the waves of the ocean;
I'll toss you around and conquer you there.
      Then I'll become a dove, soft-feathered,
      And hide myself in the fields of air.
There I shall be as the rain and lightning,
Turning you over and pressing you close.
      Then I shall be a nun with cowl and hood;
      I'll leave the world, for the world is gross.
Gross is the world; I'll turn into parchment,
And touch you in the guise of your Book of Hours.
      If sir, you come through the convent's portal,
      You'll find me dead among the flowers.

—ballad from Mexican California

This is one of the traditional ballads mentioned in the Peralta family papers of the early 1800s. European music must have begun in the East Bay not long after Luis Peralta built his ranch house here in 1820. There would, of course, have been liturgical music as well as a rich tradition of *corridos, decimas,* and *coplas,* song traditions that go back, in some cases, to the Arab Spain of the Middle Ages. Throughout the territories of Mexico, in the Southwest, and in California, they fused with local Indian traditions. There is, in the Smithsonian, a Christmas song from the Texas borderlands made up of an Andalusian tune and a chorus in the language of the Cheyennes. "O Blanca Virgin," a witty and flirtatious duet, is a very old song.

235

MY DARLING CLEMENTINE

In a cabin, in a canyon,
Excavating for a mine,
Dwelt a miner, Forty-niner,
And his daughter Clementine.

Drove her ducklings to the river
Every morning just at nine,
Stubbed her toe against a sliver,
Fell into the foaming brine.

Ruby lips above the water,
Blowing bubbles soft and fine,
But alas she was no swimmer,
And I lost my Clementine.

Oh my darling, oh my darling,
Oh my darling Clementine,
You are lost and gone forever,
Dreadful sorry, Clementine.

—Percy Montrose

The sheet music for "My Darling Clementine" was first published by the Oliver Ditson Company in Boston in 1884. The author is identified as one **Percy Montrose,** about whom nothing is known. UC Berkeley's Bancroft Library, with its wealth of documents for the study of California history, houses an extensive collection of sheet music from the gold rush years and after. Berkeley, of course, did not yet exist in 1849, the year of the gold rush the song commemorates; it was still part of the Peralta ranch, a hillside of grasslands and wooded canyons sloping to the bay, through which Strawberry and Cordonices Creeks flowed. The immediate effect of mining on the landscape of the East Bay was the clear-cutting of the hills. The price of redwood lumber in 1847 was thirty dollars per one thousand board feet, a price that leapt to six hundred per thousand square feet by the end of 1849. With the introduction of steam sawmills, the thousand-year-old redwood forests of the Oakland and Berkeley hills disappeared like Clementine.

CHECK YOURSELF

You better check yourself, don't know what you're doing
You better check yourself, 'cause you don't know what you're doing
I see something in the making and ain't nothing but some trouble brewing

You take Friday, Saturday, Sunday, too
You never home, what you trying to do?
Check yourself, don't know what you're doing
I see something in the making and nothing but trouble brewing

Well, I've told you once, told you twice
You can't run around baby, be my wife
Check yourself, don't know what you're doing
I see something in the making and nothing but trouble brewing

Riding high, flying low, it's time for me to go
Riding high, flying low, it's time for me to go
I'm going to leave this town, I ain't coming home no more
Better check yourself, don't know what you're doing
Better check yourself 'cause you don't know what you're doing
I see something in the making and nothing but some trouble brewing

—Lowell Fulson

Lowell Fulson (1921–1999), the leading figure in the emergence of the Oakland blues scene, was born on a Choctaw Indian reservation in Oklahoma and grew up playing gospel and country music. During World War II he served in the U.S. Navy in Oakland and stayed on to play music in clubs, beginning his recording career in 1946. In the war years the African American population of the East Bay swelled with servicemen and defense-plant and shipyard workers, mostly migrants from Texas and Louisiana. Fulson played blues and rhythm and blues to the new audiences in the Oakland clubs. His songs were sung by Elvis Presley, Otis Redding, and B. B. King. He won five W. C. Handy Awards and is a member of the Blues Hall of Fame. He died in Long Beach, California.

THIS WORLD

Baby, I ain't afraid to die,
It's just that I hate to say goodbye
To this world, this world, this world.
This old world is mean and cruel,
But still I love it like a fool,
This world, this world, this world.

I'd rather go to the corner store
Than sing hosannah on that golden shore,
I'd rather live on Parker Street
Than fly around where the angels meet.
Oh, this old world is all I know,
It's dust to dust when I have to go
From this world, this world, this world.

Somebody else will take my place,
Some other hands, some other face,
Some other eyes will look around
And find the things I've never found
Don't weep for me when I am gone,
Just keep this old world rolling on,
This world, this world, this world.

—Malvina Reynolds

Malvina Reynolds (1900–1978) was born in San Francisco and received a BA, MA, and PhD in English from UC Berkeley. In the 1920s her friends were the poets and writers among the students, including the visiting Tennessean Robert Penn Warren, Ruth Witt-Diamant, who went on to found the Poetry Center at San Francisco State, and Carolyn Anspacher, for many years a writer for the *San Francisco Chronicle*. During the 1930s Reynolds taught in the Oakland public schools, but lost her job because of her political views. She also held jobs as an assembly-line worker, a tailor, and a social worker. She began writing songs in the late 1940s and early 1950s, when the folk music revival in the United States was just getting underway. Her earliest songs were published in *Sing Out!,* the leading magazine of the folk music movement. "Little Boxes" was recorded by Pete Seegar, and "What Have They Done to the Rain" by The Searchers. Soon her songs were being sung by Woodie Guthrie, Bob Dylan, Joan Baez, Judy Collins, and Harry Belafonte. From the mid-1960s into the 1970s she performed her own songs in the United States and all over the world. Though she got started when she was almost fifty, she wrote, all told, more than five hundred songs. "This World" was one of her favorites.

PUFF THE MAGIC DRAGON

Puff the magic dragon lived by the sea
And frolicked in the autumn mist in a land called Honah Lee,
Little Jackie Paper loved that rascal Puff,
And brought him strings and sealing wax and other fancy stuff.

Together they would travel on a boat with billowed sail,
Jackie kept a lookout perched on Puff's gigantic tail,
Noble kings and princes would bow whenever they came,
Pirate ships would lower their flag when Puff roared out his name.

A dragon lives forever but not so little boys,
Painted wings and giant rings make way for other toys.
One grey night it happened, Jackie Paper came no more
And Puff that mighty dragon, he ceased his fearless roar.

His head was bent in sorrow, green scales fell like rain,
Puff no longer went to play along the cherry lane.
Without his life-long friend, Puff could not be brave,
So Puff that mighty dragon sadly slipped into his cave.

Oh! Puff the magic dragon lived by the sea
And frolicked in the autumn mist in a land called Honah Lee,
Puff the magic dragon lived by the sea
And frolicked in the autumn mist in a land called Honah Lee.

—Lenny Lipton

242

Lenny Lipton was born in Brooklyn, New York, in 1940 and attended Cornell University. In 1965 he moved to Berkeley, where he became the film critic for that era's quintessential underground newspaper, the *Berkeley Barb*, produced films, wrote a book *(Independent Filmmaking)* and was a regular contributor to *The Realist* magazine. He also received an award from the Smithsonian Museum for his pioneering work in the electronic stereoscopic display industry and became CEO of StereoGraphics Corporation. Nevertheless he is perhaps best known for having written the song "Puff the Magic Dragon" in 1959. By the time he arrived in Berkeley, it had been set to music by Peter Yarrow of the folk group Peter, Paul, and Mary, and become a popular children's song and a favorite of those interested in magical states of mind. Lipton now lives in Greenbrae his wife, three children, five birds, six fish, and one dog.

I-FEEL-LIKE-I'M-FIXIN'-TO-DIE RAG

Come on all of you big strong men,
Uncle Sam needs your help again.
He's got himself in a terrible jam
Way down yonder in Vietnam
So put down your books and pick up a gun,
We're gonna have a whole lotta fun.

Come on mothers throughout the land,
Pack your boys off to Vietnam.
Come on fathers, don't hesitate,
Send your sons off before it's too late.
You can be the first one on your block
To have your boy come home in a box.

And it's one, two, three,
What are we fighting for?
Don't ask me, I don't give a damn,
Next stop is Vietnam;
And it's five, six, seven,
Open up the pearly gates,
Well there ain't no time to wonder why,
Whoopee! we're all gonna die.

—Joe McDonald

Joe McDonald was born in Washington, D.C., in 1942 and his family moved to California when he was three years old. He studied music in grade school, and in high school in Los Angeles County he became student director of the school band. He discovered rock and roll as a teen-ager and gave up plans to pursue a classical music career. After three years in the U.S. Navy, he returned to California for college, but soon dropped out. He moved to Berkeley to become a folk singer, where he published a "zine" called *Rag Baby,* performed jug band music with The Berkeley String Quartet, and, in 1965, wrote the "I-Feel-Like-I'm-Fixin'-to-Die Rag." He produced a small record with his now-famous song on it for a "talking issue" of his magazine and sold it at a UC Berkeley teach-in on the Vietnam War. Shortly thereafter his band became Country Joe and the Fish and his song the anthem of the Vietnam War protest movement. Though he has performed all over the world, he continues to live in Berkeley, where he produces music on the Rag Baby label. He designed the City of Berkeley Vietnam Veterans Memorial at the Veterans Memorial Building.

KNOWLEDGE

I know that things are getting tougher
When you can't get the top off from the bottom of the barrel.
Wide open road of my future now...
It's looking fucking narrow.
All I know is that I don't know nothing.
We get told to decide.
Just like as if I'm not going to change my mind.
All I know is that I don't know nothing.
Whatcha gonna do with yourself,
Boy better make up your mind...
Whatcha gonna do with yourself,
You're running out of time.
This time I got it all figured out:
All I know is that I don't know nothing.
And that's fine.

    —Jesse Michaels and Tim Armstrong, Operation Ivy

Jesse Michaels and **Tim Armstrong** were the lead singer and guitarist of the Berkeley punk band Operation Ivy. Known for playing an exuberant combination of punk and ska, Operation Ivy's lyrics mixed political and social commentary with personal experience and outraged idealism. During its brief existence, the band released one album, *Energy* (1989), and after the breakup the group grew into legend and *Energy* achieved gold record status in 2003. Operation Ivy was a head-liner in an underground music scene that flourished among the young in Berkeley in the 1980s. The scene was centered on 924 Gilman, a community-run club that opened its doors at about the same time the band came together. Both the band and the club belonged to a moment when it seemed the youth could take control of the musical culture that was being mass-marketed at them.

A GIFT

For a long time now I have not been able to listen
to Dinu Lipatti's slender, ascetic fingertips
pressing ever so gently firm on the piano keys

in his last recorded transcription of Bach's Cantata
"Jesus bleibet meine Freude" given to me
by George Oppen the year he died.

    It is too sad to hear
that severe, geometrically measured stroll of the soul
healthily light-stepping into heaven,

and has become sadder with each loved one's death:
the slow, spare, stately pace wrenching the heart
with its grateful ascendancy over grief,

and staring as if straight into the face of God
either everywhere or nowhere, leaving us
nothing to say, nothing to hear as luminous

and meltingly tender as the air
fills with silence, and the heart with loss.

    —Jack Marshall

Jack Marshall was born in Brooklyn in 1936. After graduating from high school, he worked in New York's Garment District, then traveled in the South and the Midwest, working in a canning factory, a steel mill, as a migrant laborer, and as a deckhand on a Norwegian freighter bound for Africa. After he returned to New York, he married and became part of the poetry scene in Manhattan's Lower East Side. He published his first book, *The Darkest Continent*, there in 1967, the year before he moved to San Francisco, where he worked for twelve years as an administrative assistant to the chief of medicine at UCSF. He has twice received the Bay Area Book Reviewers Award for poetry, most recently for *Gorgeous Chaos*. He lives in El Cerrito.

THE IMPOSSIBLE POEM

Climbing the peak of Tamalpais the loose
Gravel underfoot

And the city shining with the tremendous wrinkles
In the hills and the winding of the bay
Behind it, it faces the bent ocean

Streetcars
Rocked thru the city and the winds
Combed their clumsy sides
In clumsy times

Sierras withering
Behind the storefronts

And sanity the roadside weed
Dreams of sports and sportsmanship

In the lucid towns paralyzed
Under the truck tires
Shall we relinquish

Sanity to redeem
Fragments and fragmentary
Histories in the towns and the temperate streets
Too shallow still to drown in or to mourn
The courageous and precarious children.

—George Oppen

George Oppen (1908–1984) played no direct part in the literary life of Berkeley, but he was a figure of enormous importance for poetry in the Bay Area. He was born in New Rochelle, New York, and moved as a boy to San Francisco, where his father had acquired a chain of movie theaters. He left college at Oregon State University when he and his future wife, Mary, got suspended for staying out past curfew. They traveled to New York, where they met the poet Louis Zukofsky and together established the Objectivist Press in 1933, which printed their own work and work by the poets they admired of the older generation, including William Carlos Williams and Ezra Pound. After participating in a strike of renters who, in those deep years of the Depression, were being evicted in great numbers, he joined the Communist Party and worked for ten years as a political activist, including a stint as an organizer and factory worker on a production line in Detroit. During World War II he volunteered for service as an infantryman and served in Germany and France. After the war he and his wife traveled to Mexico to avoid the McCarthy years. He worked as a furniture maker and, having set aside poetry in 1933 to work for political change, he took it up again in the late 1950s and published his first book in thirty years, *The Materials,* in 1962. His next book, *Of Being Numerous,* received the Pulitzer Prize in 1969. In 1966 the Oppens moved from Brooklyn to San Francisco, where they opened their home to young Bay Area poets and were an admired and vivid presence in the city. After her husband's death, Mary, author of a memoir about their years together entitled *Meaning a Life,* moved to the Thousand Oaks neighborhood and continued to offer conversation and hospitality to young writers until her death in 1990.

PIANO MAN

Friday night. Beautiful jazz piano at Picante's. Two people in
the room. Three grubby skateboarders and several ticket
holders waiting for their food in the next. The music, simple,
yet impossibly lovely, impossibly complicated, pours out of
the shiny black spinet. The piano player notices me listening.
He can hear me listening. He turns his head slightly to look.
I look away to avoid eye contact because the music is
impossibly intimate. How can I tell him that it's okay that no
one but me hears? That I will walk out and down Sixth Street
and he will be alone but that he must not stop playing? That
he is not alone as long as he sounds? That he means as long as
he sounds? That he cannot stop playing. He must not.

—Joyce Jenkins

Joyce Jenkins is the editor of *Poetry Flash,* Berkeley's monthly literary calendar and poetry review, which has grown from its founding in 1972 as a mimeograph calendar of Bay Area poetry readings to its present role as a quarterly West Coast literary review and calendar in a tabloid format with a circulation of 22,000. Jenkins was born in Ypsilanti, Michigan, in 1952 and went to Wayne State and Grand Valley State Universities in Michigan. Already passionately involved in poetry, she came to San Francisco in the mid 1970s and took an apartment on Haight Street. She moved to Berkeley in 1976 and began to help coordinate the weekly reading series at Cody's Books on Telegraph Avenue. With Steve Abbott, she took over editorship of *Poetry Flash* in 1978 and has been, as its editor and publisher (since 1980) and as a coordinator at Cody's, a central and enabling presence on the Berkeley literary scene for over twenty-five years. She was an early member of the Bay Area Book Reviewers Association and editor of the California Poetry Series at Heyday Books. She was a director of the San Francisco International Poetry Festivals in 1978 and 1980 and presented poetry programs on KPFA radio in the 1980s. In 1995 she received the National Poetry Association's award for distinguished service to poetry and poets. Her chapbook, *Portal*, was published in 1993. In 1994 she received an American Book Award from the Before Columbus Foundation, and in 1996 she was honored by the National Women's Political Caucus for her contribution to "the enrichment of our literary and political lives."

THE AUDIENCE

Redemption? because they loved me? or loved me in my words?
   intelligent faces soulful pricked for the poetry

   And that night a woman came in a dream   Indian or black
aging alone the phrase "ghosts in her eyes"
     "I'm a perfect case for attention," she said
  So I was listening to her words pained dry fretful driven
writing them down for the poetry   that disappears
     She seemed flattered not realizing
  the flat of the language   its tundra
   I was flattered too not realizing her own need
       simply to speak
    "Loaves of bread," she said

    The next morning I saw   loaves were love risen
their faces amazed that we know someone in dreams
   wandering in tundra   redeemed

   —Richard Silberg

254

Richard Silberg was born in Brooklyn in 1940 and hitchhiked across the country from Cambridge, Massachusetts, to Berkeley in 1966, a trip that resulted in his first published poems. He returned to Berkeley in 1969 and has lived in California ever since. In 1978 he began working on *Poetry Flash,* joining Steve Abbott and Joyce Jenkins, who were then producing the paper. He became associate editor several years later and has curated, with Joyce Jenkins, Poetry Flash @ Cody's, the main poetry reading series in the city, for twenty years. Silberg has introduced the readings, reviewed poetry for the *Flash,* and taught a poetry workshop through UC Extension that drew students from all over the Bay Area. His books of poetry include *Translucent Gears, The Fields, Totem Pole,* and *Doubleness.* A collection of his *Poetry Flash* essays, *Reading the Sphere: A Geography of Contemporary American Poetry*, was published in 2002.

FENNEL

give the hungry
some seeds and they'll sleep full
for another day
who wants to wake to misery

i'm sister to sorrow
cousin to parsley
sometimes telling the truth is too painful
i flatter
an ugly woman
you look good enough to eat
what is a false compliment
in comparison to a hurt feeling

mek dem slander me
fi   sow fennel   is fi sow sorrow
not true
me tall wid a head full of hair
but me beauty is de moles dem
all ova me body

the anguish you feel
cuts to the marrow
i am profound

 —Opal Palmer Adisa

Opal Palmer Adisa was born in Kingston, Jamaica, in 1954 and moved to New York in 1970 to attend Hunter College. After earning her BA, she returned to Jamaica, where she worked in the government's education office, producing and directing educational programs for both radio and television. She moved to California in 1979 to pursue graduate work in ethnic studies and education, and has published fiction, poetry, and criticism in venues ranging from *The Oxford Companion to African American Literature* to *Erotique Noir: Black Erotica.* She is the author of a children's book, *Pina, the Many-Eyed Fruit* (1985), a book of stories, *Bake-Face and Other Guava Stories* (1986), and a novel, *It Begins With Tears* (1997). Her book of poems, *Tamarind and Mango Women,* won the Josephine Miles/PEN Oakland Award in 1992. She lives in Oakland with her three children and teaches at the California College of Arts and Crafts.

PREMONITION

The owl sings
a plaintive overture
to interruption.

The burden of the scorching sun
gives way.

In the blossoms
of an ancient cactus
pure light
sketches the entrails
of history.

Its frail purple hand
trembles on the verge
of fortune:

On the thin leaf
of memory
the green lash
of time paints
cherries in tender
                    water.

From indian chalices
emerge premonitions
of absent blood.

   —Lucha Corpi, translated by Catherine Rodriguez-Nieto

Lucha Corpi was born in 1945 in the village of Jaltipan, Veracruz, in Mexico, where she received most of her formal education. In 1964 she married and came to Berkeley "at the onset," she has written, "of the most exciting but turbulent decade in the history of Berkeley." She enrolled in McKinley High School's English for Foreign Born program and later attended Merritt College. In 1967 her son was born, and two years later she and her husband divorced. "Partly because I found myself alone in a new country," she wrote, "I turned to the writing of poetry." While attending UC Berkeley, she worked part-time as a bilingual secretary on campus and became involved with the Chicano civil rights movement. She graduated from Berkeley with a degree in comparative literature and has worked as a teacher in the Oakland public schools' Adult Education Program for twenty years, during which time she has also earned an MA in comparative literature from San Francisco State. Her poetry is written in Spanish, her fiction in English, "a language I have spoken for most of my adult life but still feels like seawater, tears and blood, on my tongue."

CORRIDO BLANCO

Her notebook declares, "If for you fathers
my logos suffers too, (what did Paul say?)
'Mulieres' You 'in Ecclesia tace-
ant.' Too, mujeres en iglesia, you

te nacen, palabrita, tú, mía."
In the schools from Rome, you are born living,
from London too: nace la palabra.
And you become and kill a tongue or two.

Criolla, woman whose words I see, hear,
maestra, teacher, eye and ear and tongue
for me. Here I am one nine year old boy.
No hay razón, sólo poder. Here I

hear, see, palabra suya, "Know: children
be silent in school. No language, or word
or sound you know from homelands. Ameri-
ca, no way to spell it but one. I know."

   —Alfred Arteaga

Alfred Arteaga was born in Los Angeles in 1950 and studied at UC Santa Cruz. In 1989 he came to Berkeley to teach at the university. He has written several books of poetry, including *Cantos, Love in a Time of Aftershocks,* and *Red;* a volume of creative nonfiction, *The House with the Blue Bed;* and two volumes of criticism and theory, *An Other Tongue* and *Chicano Poetics.* This poem, whose title might be translated as "White Ballad," comes from his first book, *Cantos.* It takes as its subject the first poet of the Americas, Sor Juana Inés de la Cruz, a nun who wrote brilliant poetry in the court of sixteenth-century Mexico City before she was eventually silenced by the church. The speaker of this poem describes his acculturation in the American school system, where children are expected both to hold their tongues and to speak only in English, as analogous to the attempt to silence Sor Juana. St. Paul warned early Christian women *(mulieres)* to be silent *(taceant)* in church *(in Ecclesia);* this poem celebrates Sor Juana's resistance to that silencing. The narrator of the poem—mixing English, Spanish, Latin, and a bit of Greek—also defies the monolingualism that was imposed on Spanish-speaking children. Sor Juana stands as a model for finding your own word—*"sua palabra."*

diagonal plane of low grey white cloud moving
across the green of the ridge, invisible song
sparrow calling from scotch broom in the left
foreground
                woman on phone planning to start
embroidering shirt with scarlet "no," noting
that she is still in possession of two ears

shirtless man leaning back against a white
pillow on a stone wall, shadow of circular
orange flower moving back and forth across
brick-red plane

            Charles Tansley thinking
"women make civilization impossible," Lily
Briscoe liking his blue eyes
                        empty blue sky
reflected in nearly motionless plane below it,
cormorant flapping from the channel toward it

   —Stephen Ratcliffe

262

Stephen Ratcliffe was born in Boston in 1948 and moved to the San Francisco Bay Area at the age of four. He went to Reed College for a year and a half, then transferred to UC Berkeley in 1968, where he studied in the English department with Elroy Bundy, Raymond Oliver, and Steven Booth. Notable events of his college years include National Guard troops marching in riot gear across Sproul Plaza and a helicopter emerging from behind the Campanile and dropping tear gas as it came across the campus. Ratcliffe has written several books of poetry, including *Portraits & Repetitions* and *SOUND/(system),* and a collection of essays, *Listening to Reading*. He lives in Bolinas and teaches at Mills College in Oakland, where he is the director of the creative writing program.

ONE

divides	forever.
apparently twinned	identically gened
growing and changing	floating and tumbling,
sharing the prelude	entwining the other.
hearing before words	touching before hands.
Born whole.	Born apart.
Searching for	each missing

HA   LF

—John Roberts

John Roberts is the architect of the Addison Street poetry project. He was born in 1945 in Evanston, Illinois, the unexpected second-born of a pair of identical twins. After graduating from Williams College in Massachusetts with a degree in economics, he became a modern dancer in New York City and, for a brief time, a banker. He moved to Berkeley in 1971 to attend graduate school in landscape architecture and stayed on to raise a family. He maintains a Bay Area landscape architecture practice and teaches occasionally at UC Berkeley's College of Environmental Design. Moved by the hostility experienced by his children in downtown Berkeley and the deterioration of the downtown environment in the early 1980s, he committed himself to the creation of a commons at the center of Berkeley. Among his many urban design projects in downtown are the sidewalk and street improvements in the Addison Street Arts District. His poem "One" was written as a twin's reflection on shared experience.

THE BOX

When I see driven nails I think of the hammer and the hand,
his mood, the weather, the time of year, what he packed
for lunch, how built-up was the house,
the neighborhood, could he see another job from here?

And where was the lumber stacked, in what closet
stood the nail kegs, where did the boss unroll
the plans, which room was chosen for lunch? And where
did the sun strike first? Which wall cut the wind?

What was the picture in his mind as the hammer
hit the nail? A conversation? Another joke, a cigarette
or Friday, getting drunk, a woman, his wife, his youngest
kid or a side job he planned to make ends meet?

Maybe he just pictured the nail,
the slight swirl in the center of the head and raised
the hammer, and brought it down with fury and with skill
and sank it with a single blow.

Not a difficult trick for a journeyman, no harder
than figuring stairs or a hip-and-valley roof
or staking out a lot, but neither is a house,
a house is just a box fastened with thousands of nails.

 —Mark Turpin

The son of a Presbyterian minister, **Mark Turpin** was born in Berkeley at Alta Bates Hospital and attended Berkeley High from 1969 to 1971, when he wasn't participating in the many street demonstrations of the period—against the Vietnam War and the closure of People's Park. He has worked for twenty-five years as a master carpenter and crew foreman; after the Oakland–Berkeley hills fire of 1991, he participated, along with carpenters from around the state, in rebuilding that devastated area. A student of Robert Pinsky, he received an MA in English (without having earned a BA first) from Boston University at the age of forty-seven. His book of poems about the construction trades, *Hammer*, was published in 2003.

TEMPLE OF THE MARIPOSA

We have seen what simplicity can do.
At the very base of the ledge is a set of stairs
which lead us back down again.   The fields
overridden by weeds
choke our abandoned platform.
We know the reclaimers
and their inability to think above noise and mineral.
Up on the lintel, we carve in the shape of an ash.
And then invisible snow.
By the edge we thought there was a pool beneath us.
What is horrible in this mechanism
is the sound of its attachment.   When the descent stops,
the absence irritates us.
Steal, then, and return the green of the mediation.
Return to us the pool while it rolls down the stair.
Affection is steep but not complicated.
And the angles.   And reverence of highways.
We have adoration
of struggle—And the bridge
scratched off underground paintings.

—Elizabeth Robinson

Elizabeth Robinson was born in 1961 in Denver, Colorado. She grew up in southern California and came to Berkeley in the early 1990s as a student at the Pacific School of Religion, where she received a master's degree in divinity. She curates a summer poetry reading series in her Berkeley backyard, and with other local poets co-edits *26 Magazine,* EtherDome Press, and Instance Press. Her books include *In the Sequence of Falling Things, Bed of Lists, House Made of Silver, Harrow, Pure Descent,* and *Apprehend.*

FERAL FLOATS THE FORM IN HEAVEN AND OF LIGHT

The famous and the dead have learned to fall between our eyes
And their forms in heaven: a philosophical eclipse
Which edges them in light, like bodies in the nineteenth century
Photo plates enwrapped in their emanations and pale shrouds.
They have their own cities called Necropolis and New York
Built of what they are said to have said, the famous and the dead.
In your gleaming imitations where the density of things
Howls through the evening's blue precincts you hurry home
To practice passing drinks from mouth to mouth, you the mere,
The living, lit only by a faint electricity whose mind is elsewhere.
You wrote of them often, kissed one once, there is a picture
Of you in your chair at the end of the century, thinking their cities
Until an aura and awfulness surrounded you, a motion appearing
As no motion at all, the inverse of a wave, a demonology—

—Joshua Clover

Joshua Clover was born in Berkeley in 1962. His mother was a student and then a professor at the university, and the family lived on the corner of Fulton and Stuart. Clover attended Boston University and the Iowa Writers' Workshop. He has spent time in New York City and Paris and has lived in Berkeley on and off "in," he writes, "more than twenty different houses....Because I moved so much, I often kept a box at the main post office on Allston Street. I would sit on the steps and read my mail every day, in amongst the Berkeley High students ditching class with their brightly dyed hair. I wrote several poems sitting there in which the city of Berkeley is called "Zone"—Later I discovered Apollinaire had used the same term for another bright city." That's Guillaume Apollinaire (1880–1918), friend of the cubist painters, author of 'Zone,' a poem about Paris and one of the first great poems of the twentieth century. Clover published a book of poetry, *Madonna anno domini*, in 1997 and a book on the film *The Matrix* in 2004. He writes about music, film, and literature for the *Village Voice* and teaches English at UC Davis.

PERMISSIONS

Ursula K. Le Guin. "The Child on the Shore" from *Hard Words and Other Poems* by Ursula K. Le Guin. Copyright © 1981 by Ursula K. Le Guin. Reprinted by permission of HarperCollins Publishers Inc.

Denise Levertov. Excerpt from "Notebook: October '68–May '69" ([excerpt] Thursday, May 15th, 1959—Berkeley) from *Relearning the Alphabet,* copyright © 1970 by Denise Levertov. Reprinted by permission of New Directions Publishing Corp.

Lenny Lipton. "Puff the Magic Dragon" copyright © 1963 by Lenny Lipton. Reprinted by permission of the author.

Li Po. "Drinking Alone with the Moon" from *The Jade Mountain: A Chinese Anthology, Being Three Hundred Poems of the T'ang Dynasty, 616–906* by Li Po, translated by Witter Bynner with Kiang Kang-Hu. Copyright © 1929 by Witter Bynner. Reprinted by permission of The Witter Bynner Foundation for Poetry, Inc.

Ron Loewinsohn. "Siv, with Ocean (Pacific)" copyright © 2003 by Ron Loewinsohn. Reprinted by permission of the author.

Jack London. "Triolet" from *Martin Eden.* New York: Random House, 2002.

Osip Mandelstam. "[Sleeplessness. Homer. The sails tight.]" from *Osip Mandelstam's Stone* by Osip Mandelstam, translated by Robert Tracy. Translation copyright © 1981 by Robert Tracy. Reprinted by permission of Princeton University Press, Princeton, NJ.

Jack Marshall. "A Gift" from *Gorgeous Chaos: New and Selected Poems 1965–2001* by Jack Marshall. Copyright © 1993 by Jack Marshall. Reprinted with the permission of Coffee House Press, Minneapolis, Minnesota, USA, www.coffeehousepress.com.

Michael McClure. "Song" from *Fragments of Perseus,* copyright © 1983 by Michael McClure. Reprinted by permission of New Directions Publishing Corp.

Joe McDonald. "I-Feel-Like-I'm-Fixin'-to-Die Rag" copyright © 2002 by Joe McDonald. Reprinted by permission of the author.

David Meltzer. "For Jack Spicer" from *Arrows* by David Meltzer. Copyright © 1991 by David Meltzer. Reprinted by permission of the author.

Josephine Miles. "Reason" from *Collected Poems 1930–1983* by Josephine Miles. Copyright © 1983 by Josephine Miles. Reprinted by permission of University of Illinois Press.

Adam David Miller. "The Eye Behind the I" copyright © 2004 by Adam David Miller. Reprinted by permission of the author.

Czeslaw Milosz. "Encounter" from *The Collected Poems 1931–1987* by Czeslaw Milosz. Copyright © 1988 by Czeslaw Milosz Royalties, Inc. Reprinted by permission of HarperCollins Publishers Inc.

Percy Montrose. "My Darling Clementine." Oliver Ditson & Co., 1884.

INDEX